Revealing
Illustrations

REVEALING ILLUSTRATIONS
The Art of James McMullan

With an Introductory Interview
by Milton Glaser

Watson-Guptill Publications, New York

First published 1981 in New York by Watson-Guptill Publications,
a division of Billboard Publications, Inc.,
1515 Broadway, New York, N.Y. 10036

Library of Congress Cataloging in Publication Data

McMullan, James, 1934–
  Revealing illustrations.

  Includes index.
  1. McMullan, James, 1934–
2. Commercial art—Technique. I. Title.
NC999.4.M38A4   1981   741.6'092'4   81–7450
ISBN 0–8230–4549–8   AACR2

Manufactured in Japan

First Printing, 1981

1 2 3 4 5 6 7 8 9/86 85 84 83 82 81

197620

For George, for Katy, and for Leigh

Acknowledgments

My deepest gratitude to Michele Kubick for her incredible work organizing the material and for all her perceptions and support throughout the project; also to Richard Mantel for his crucial advice on the design of the book. To my editors, Michael McTwigan and Betty Vera—Michael, particularly for his enthusiasm and his ideas; Betty, for her always clarifying editing and her calmness. I am also grateful to Marsha Melnick for her faith in the book from the start.

Contents

Milton Glaser Interviews James McMullan

This interview with James McMullan was conducted by Milton Glaser in New York on two occasions in April and May of 1981.

MG: When did you decide to become an illustrator? In my own case, there was a very specific moment when I was about four or five years old. My cousin came in with a paper bag and said, "You want to see a pigeon?" I thought he had one in the bag, but he didn't. Right before my eyes, he just drew it on the paper bag. At that moment the idea of inventing an image—it was the first time it had ever occurred to me that you could invent something and give it life—became clear. That was the moment of decision for me, and I never deviated from that. The only thing I ever wanted to do was something involved with making images. Did you have a similar moment, a kind of illumination, when an internal decision was made that directed you toward this activity?

JM: That's a wonderful story. I do remember my grandmother's reaction to a drawing of Bambi I did, which I had copied right out of a Walt Disney book—it was quite a hit. I was about seven at the time, and as far as my grandmother was concerned, I became an artist right then and there. Actually, I think that my focusing on art also had a lot to do with my solitariness as a kid and the fact that I spent a great deal of time watching things from the sidelines. I was isolated because during World War II, my mother and I traveled from China to Canada, then to India, and back to China. I think that lonely kids often get involved with drawing or writing, and in my case, drawing became connected with my watching things. I was drawing Bambis and killer submarines and all the things that boys imagine, but I also remember doing drawings of my schoolmaster in which I would try to get the effect of his black robe, which to me was awesome. I think I was trying to control threatening things in the world by making drawings of them. It's probably as reasonable a beginning for an illustrator as any other.

MG: But what model did you have? Where did the idea of being artistic come from?

JM: My father was a musician and could play several musical instruments, and so I'm sure I saw him as an artistic person. One of my few distinct memories from the years before we left China the first time—I would have been five or six years old—is that he would come home in the late afternoon and sit down at this grand piano we had and play and sing. He often sang "The Way You Look Tonight," and he always seemed particularly happy to me at those times.

MG: In this same early period, were there also influences that affected your idea of what art was about?

JM: Actually, as I think of that room where my father played the piano, I can visualize the walls—they were covered with Chinese painted scrolls—and I know this art had an enormous effect on me. The paintings had a lot of Chinese writing on them, and I kept thinking that the calligraphy was as beautiful as the painting. I remember watching one of the servants writing a letter home, and I was fascinated by the way he held the brush and flicked it around to make the characters. I already knew that drawing was important to me, really any kind of drawing, because when I later went to a boarding school in Darjeeling, I discovered comic books—American comic books. They were very exotic and exciting to us English boys, and we tried to make drawings of the characters that looked just like the originals. I was okay at it, but there was one kid who had really perfected a copy of this Wonder Woman kind of character, and we all looked up to him as the Master. I think I got a glimpse of the sort of attention art might bring you if you could do it well enough.

MG: I am convinced that the model for most painters and artists of our generation was the comics. For artists who have grown up during the last fifty years, copying the comics is almost the equivalent of the Academy. That's the way everybody I know started. I certainly started that way. All I ever wanted to do was be a comic-strip artist—quite precisely, because of the rewards of that activity. If you could copy Dick Tracy or Donald Duck accurately, you were very much rewarded by your peers who couldn't do it. Then you graduated to drawing naked girls for them. But I think it would be amusing if someone did research on how comics have formed not only the basic training mechanism for young artists in America, but also the means by which their earliest approval is guaranteed.

Anyway, once you identified that there was something special to this activity, some reward and distinction, and also that you seemed to have an aptitude for doing it, what happened? What was your earliest use of that understanding?

JM: Probably some posters I did in sixth grade that had very neat lettering, as I remember them. They won a local prize, but it may have been for correct spelling and clean edges—I don't think they were very imaginative. Mostly, realistic subjects interested me at that time. Except for a brief period of copying comics, I wasn't intrigued, as many kids are, by drawing monsters and imaginary subjects. The art I did that I can remember was somewhat stiff. I think I was trying to make some impossible connection between the things I was seeing in real life and the Chinese paintings on the walls at home.

MG: Did the possibility of being an illustrator occur to you at that time?

JM: I think it did, because I remember being fascinated with the covers and inside illustrations of the *Saturday Evening Post*. I was very affected by the mood of the pictures, and I think that my fundamental attitude toward illustration was formed at that time. I'm fairly certain that seeing the *Saturday Evening Post* on a regular basis provided my first glimpse of illustration as a real occupation. I started to daydream about making drawings and paintings like the ones in the magazine. Of course, I looked at other magazines and followed the work of Boris Artzybasheff and Chaliapin on *Time* covers and so on. By the time I began high school, I had decided that the regular art classes were not enough for me—I guess I had made my decision to become an illustrator—and so I started studying art with a painter who lived on Salt Spring Island in Canada, where I was at the time. His name was Plato Ustinov—he was Peter Ustinov's uncle. At that time I also decided to teach myself sho-card lettering—you know, the method of rolling a chisel-edged brush in your fingers to make letters of a consistent width in one stroke. I got quite good at it and was able to make money doing posters and signs. I was very busy making sale signs for grocery stores and, at the same time, taking lessons in high art from a Russian aristocrat. Maybe you can see the whole dichotomy of my life right there.

MG: What kind of professional school did you think you would go to, or did you have other plans?

JM: In 1951, right after I graduated from high school, my mother and I moved to Seattle, Washington, and I went to a school called the Cornish School of Allied Arts, where I studied illustration until I went into the army a year later. After a two-year hitch in the army in North Carolina, I came to New York and enrolled at Pratt Institute. Apart from studying with Richard Lindner and meeting a few talented students, my years at Pratt were not my best. I seemed to be out of tune with the institution. I think I realized that I probably should have gone to a good liberal arts college at this point in my life. I was much more interested and creative, in a way, in my liberal arts subjects than I was in my art classes.

MG: Do you think if you had gone to a liberal arts college that you might have gone in a very different direction? Or, more precisely, could you have become a painter at that point, as opposed to an illustrator? Or did you have some very clear idea in your mind of some relationship between literary ideas and graphic ideas that you wanted to explore?

JM: I don't know how clear it was, but, yes, I had a feeling that there was an important link between literary and graphic ideas that intrigued me. As for being a painter, I think because of the kind of painting that was being done then—Abstract Expressionism—it was hard for me to work up any enthusiasm for the idea of myself as a painter. I was simply too interested in what I believed to be the high possibilities of figurative art, particularly in the context of illustration. This was what spurred me on in that period.

MG: It's true that in the early fifties, it seemed impossible to do figurative work in painting and the only legitimate recourse for figurative work appeared to be illustration. I know that in my own case, I never had any painting aspirations at all—but I always felt there was a serious body of work to be done in either illustration or design that was not a reduced version of painting but had its own objectives, its own effects, and its own intentions. I know you share this. But in the area of illustration, I imagine certain models were beginning to emerge for you at that point. What were they, and what were some of the other models that influenced you at different points in your career? Sometimes you can see the development of a career just by virtue of the change in what one admires.

JM: In those days of reading the *Saturday Evening Post* at my uncle's house on Salt Spring Island, I was very enthusiastic about Norman Rockwell. I liked the way he used body language to suggest character. Later on I discovered Robert Fawcett. Probably because Fawcett was basically a draftsman, he had a special meaning for me. I read somewhere that he drew his whole picture in black and gray ink and then tinted the image in color. For years I was intrigued with using ink because of Fawcett. I liked the fact that his pictures weren't illusionistic in the same sense that Rockwell's pictures were; in Fawcett's work you could see the process—you could see that they were essentially drawings.

MG: I remember seeing an original of his at the Society of Illustrators when I was a teenager—like yourself, I have always admired him—and I was absolutely amazed. For one thing, it was a very complex work—his often were. You remember that he did a series of illustrations of Sherlock Holmes stories?

JM: Yes.

MG: They were very carefully studied in terms of the furniture of the period, the dinnerware, what kind of lamp was on the table, and so on. Fawcett worked in a traditional illustrative way, recreating a setting almost as if he were doing a movie set, and then lighting and photographing it . . . all very scrupulously done in terms of attention to detail, and with enormous skill as a draftsman. At the same time, his illustrations have a fluid quality; they are not at all labored, which is surprising in combination with those other attributes. I remember seeing the original illustration and being absolutely dazzled by the sureness and the ease of the brush handling. I suspect it's one of the things you admired most—the extraordinary facility and grace that came from the way he used the brush. Some of the works have quite a remarkable degree of illusion, considering that most of them were really toned wash drawings.

JM: You're absolutely right. The connection between the two might seem strange, but I think Fawcett's brushwork brought my interest in Chinese calligraphy up to date. Fawcett's work showed me a contemporary way of using that same energy.

Another illustrator I liked because he seemed so modern at the time was Al Parker. I thought his work was very audacious in its use of big blank spaces and its emphasis on patterning. I don't feel quite the same way about it now. At a certain point, the persistent fashionableness of Parker's figures became boring to me. But for a time he influenced my attitude toward composing a picture, setting things off to the side, and so forth.

Actually, because so much of the illustration of the fifties began to seem thin, a few of the illustration students at Pratt, including myself, became enamored of several figurative painters who had established themselves before Abstract Expressionism. Ben Shahn, Max Beckmann, Picasso, Ernest Kirchner, Giorgio Morandi are the names I remember. I think what attracted us to these artists was their passion and expressiveness and, of course, the fact that they were making figurative pictures. I think you could see the influence of these artists—Beckmann and the others—in some of the illustration of the early sixties. Ironically, you often saw this illustration in "girlie" magazines like *Escapade* and *Nugget*. As you remember, we had free creative reign in these publications because the editors didn't really care what we did with the illustrations. With photos of naked women in the center spreads, they certainly didn't need our art to sell the magazines. So we went wild making many neo-German-Expressionist illustrations, a lot of them aggressively unattractive. It was like a catharsis to move against what we saw as the empty prettiness of big-time illustration. I hope there's still some corner of publishing where young illustrators can make interesting mistakes more or less in private.

MG: You're talking about an interesting moment that also affected me, which is the time when the *Saturday Evening Post* lost its dominance. The *Saturday Evening Post* represented a continuation of the American illustration tradition to a large extent, going from Winslow Homer to Howard Pyle to N. C. Wyeth down through Rockwell and John Falter and the whole Westport school. All those people are part of that massive and very significant illustration tradition that was then beginning to weaken, as all movements do—to run out of gas a bit, and to become increasingly less convincing. At that point it suddenly became possible for illustrators to look outside of illustration for models for their work. Although illustrators had always done

this to some extent, at that point the influence of artists like Paul Klee was dramatically evident in the design and illustration of many artists working in the magazines. Suddenly they began to turn from illustration to nontraditional painting as the basic resource.

JM: Particularly a kind of graphic painting that involved linear work and color drawing. Shahn, for instance, was a giant to all of us at that point.

MG: Shahn was very important in making us aware that there was a bridge. He was really half illustrator, half painter; he very clearly had a foot in both camps. I think that though Shahn thought of himself basically as a painter, the fact that he illustrated so much and did so many books and posters (even to the extent of being proud of his lettering), makes it impossible not to see him as one of the very significant bridges between painting and the applied arts.

JM: Also the passionate social sentiment he acknowledged in his work, which had an obvious implication for an illustrator: that it was possible to illustrate—especially serious and emotional subject matter—without necessarily losing esthetic integrity. His painting of Sacco and Vanzetti gave me more hope for what could be done in illustration than any other work I saw during those years.

MG: Absolutely. The body of his work led many of us to feel that in his heart, Shahn was concerned with telling stories and doing it at a very high level indeed. He could tell a story and he wouldn't be embarrassed by either the content of the story or the way he told it.

JM: It was very important to me then to find models for expressing literary ideas. As I look back over the years, I see that my models have shifted more and more to artists who could teach me something about painting. I don't think I could ever be really interested in a painter who I did not find expressive, but I think that the emphasis definitely has shifted to esthetics in the art I find most useful to me now. In 1974 I saw an exhibition that included most of the famous American watercolorists, and it was very clarifying to see these painters side by side. What came out of it for me was that, at that time, the work of Maurice Prendergast was confirming and encouraging a track that I was already on. That track, simply put, was a partly impressionistic approach to forms, with a great deal of emphasis on the energy and expressive power of the brushstrokes themselves. Although I have never been interested in breaking up forms as much as Prendergast did, his work has been a very helpful model for my way of working over the last few years.

MG: Why don't we talk a little about how you actually work? For instance, what is the part of the process of working that you find most thrilling and satisfying? Is there a discrete time in any job where you find that your attention is most completely engaged and you feel you are at your best?

JM: Yes, I think of it as being a moment of invention, but not the sort of invention that you might first think of. It occurs after I decide how I want to show the subject and design the big forms of the image, but it affects the way I actually carry out these first decisions. It might involve the color combinations or the specific shapes I use, a particular way of handling a transition, or some simplification of a complex form. In other words, it usually isn't finding the basic ingredients of the picture, the metaphor, the staging, and so forth, even though those things are often pleasurable. The high moment for me is some small turn that the image takes—often esthetic—which changes the image in some fundamental way for me. When it happens, I often feel that the image becomes mine.

MG: That you own it?

JM: I think that's a good way to say it. The effect of this particular moment of invention is difficult to separate from that of the more obvious first stages of inventing the picture—thinking of the basic idea and designing it—because often this later small change will alter the whole character of the image so that even the basic idea seems different. An example that might make this point clearer is what happened when I designed the poster for *Anna Christie*. The high point for me in that process was when I thought of turning the scribbly background pencil lines of a sketch into an actual painted gesture: the wild, horizontal strokes that you see develop out of the deep red color behind Anna's figure. When I tried it in the color sketch, it didn't make conceptual sense exactly, but it felt right, and it was much more exhilarating to invent and to do than thinking of the pose for the figure or the colors in the poster. Of course, it changed how everything looked, and it also led to the way I solved the problem of the lettering. But it was a crazy and gratuitous element in a sense, and, yes, it made me feel like I possessed the art—that I owned it.

MG: During the course of doing a problem, then, it is not in the choice and disposition of the elements where you feel most alive. It is when you have gotten those elements arranged and then, in the course of working, something happens that surprises you and, though it is not what you had planned, you take advantage of it.

JM: I think the fortuitous turn occurs partly because I allow for it. I have always resisted systematizing my work in a way that would block off the surprises that come up as I invent and paint the image. I think that part of my method is to walk the edges as much as possible and to stay open to whatever is new and idiosyncratic about the information in each assignment. I find that the novelty or difficulty of the illustration problem may lead me to make esthetic inventions that I might not have thought of without the assignment. Of course, this is a tricky business. Some assignments contain information that is useful and stimulating to me, and others are about subjects that leave me cold and which I must struggle to assimilate. But, by and large, I have used problem-solving in illustration as a catalyst for maturing in my work.

MG: The issue of how the problem itself in illustration or design can be nourishing for the artist is a crucial one. For you, what is the difference between an assignment that is stimulating and one that is not?

JM: When I try to define what makes a good assignment, the first thing that comes to mind is that the subject allows for a psychological edge—that is, I can give the picture a feeling of portent, that something is about to happen which may be narratively elusive but emotionally real.

MG: Explain that a little.

JM: Well, I enjoy drawing and painting figures so that they appear to have an inner life, an afterlife, and even an underlife—so that they are not stock characters from "central casting" but are complex, probably volatile inhabitants of our time and circumstances.

A good example of an assignment in which I was able to achieve such complex characterizations was the Brooklyn disco series that I did for you at *New York* magazine. The people in those pictures had levels, I think, and the job itself changed something fundamental in the way I saw my work and how it could operate within a magazine. Because I had trusted my instincts enough to work from the photographs of the disco people without changing or hyping the information, they ended up being simple images of men walking across the floor or just groups of dancers dancing—and I got to see how well images that were not action-packed looked in the magazine. From then on, I have felt freer to be simpler with my pictures and to trust that certain kinds of nuance will carry within the context of a magazine. I came to the conclusion that if I feel strongly about a subject, I don't have to conceptually manipulate it—the inherent drama will be revealed in my painting.

MG: Paradoxically, the disco pictures are illustrations in the truest sense, with a direct lineage back to Winslow Homer. To a large extent, this idea of illustration—to illuminate as accurately as possible what a text has to suggest—is no longer in style. There are very few people who do this, but it is, in fact, one of the things that you do extraordinarily. But to return for a moment to the idea of opportunity in an assignment. What else, apart from qualities of psychological complexity, represents creative opportunity for you?

JM: I need creative freedom in finding a way to solve the image. A good assignment is one in which the problem is clearly stated either by the text or by the client, who explains the objectives but gives me very little else in the way of guidelines. Not only does this offer me the freedom to invent my own solutions, but it also allows me to hook up to the information in my own way. This last point is a little elusive, but it is a very crucial one for me. I must find that place within the problem that connects to my own concerns, my own biases, my own memories, so that the inventing I eventually do is personal and, to me, exciting. A great deal of my sketching and the time I spend visually "trying on" bits and pieces of the research is really a search for that spot in the information that intrigues me or touches me or even repels me. As long as this aspect of the information has an emotional or intuitive reality for me, I can usually make something of it creatively.

MG: When you think a piece is most successful, most satisfying to you, what are the things you celebrate in it? What things in it give you the greatest satisfaction in terms of either your idea of professionalism or your use of this career as an expressive tool?

JM: I do want to be understood. I have no interest in being obscure, and it pleases me when something I have done is dramatic and effective as illustration; but there are two other qualities that are even more important to me. One is that I hope my work will be more than effective; I want it to be affecting, to seem true and therefore be emotionally touching. The second thing I hope for, which is perhaps an extension of the first, is that my work will have reverberations for the viewer as it does for me. Because of the way I experience the world myself—as a complex shifting and connecting of events and feelings—I want to create levels of allusion in my pictures. I want the subjects of my pictures to suggest more than they ostensibly do. Actually, since so much of the staging in my pictures is undramatic in the usual sense, I depend a great deal on investing commonplace subjects with implications of significance. I have never been very interested in exploiting the most obviously dramatic aspects of a subject. I invariably move to the edges and try to find my drama there.

MG: Why don't you let me propose a small theory about this? When you introduced me one evening at the Ethical Culture Society's series on graphic designers, I mentioned that I have been described as a very idiosyncratic designer and I was thrilled by the description. I have always hated the idea that someone could have control over me by fully understanding my work. Let me propose that this is not entirely alien to your own feelings: While your work exists in the world clearly as illustration—it represents a story—at the same time, just as you don't want to be judged totally by the way you look and talk and dress and what might be called surface appearances, you also want your work to suggest that there is complexity and depth and mystery to the world (and to you) that is not immediately perceptible. The surface narrative is one thing, but if the viewer presses on, he may realize that there is a second, coexisting world that is less accessible but probably even more rewarding than the one that seems to be on the surface.

JM: You're right. I don't like to be pinned down either. Perhaps I can't be pinned down. I realize that my most creative mode is a somewhat chaotic one in which I leave open many options at once, including the option to fail. It is certainly the reason my progression in many assignments is like a long road covered with the fragments of false starts and different approaches. That process of my searching out and refining conceptual and esthetic ideas is what this book is about, of course. I hope that, as the reader sees the fragments and reads about the human and circumstantial elements that helped shape my decisions, the complex and inevitable connection between the work and who I am will be revealed. I think this connection exists for any artist, but it is a truth that runs counter to a popularly held notion of professionalism in illustration—that work is accomplished through manual skill, taste, and logic alone.

MG: I so often love the preliminary work and the early drawings and the developmental stages of a project, and I know that for myself, I wouldn't take it any farther; but you always seem to press on toward some other purpose, some other effect. I can't always tell, from my point of view, why you abandon certain ideas and go farther with certain others.

JM: The practical reasons are the easiest to describe; often, the sketches don't contain enough detail to satisfy the narrative demands of the assignment. They are really formal esthetic investigations of the whole picture. Also, I am usually trying to figure out something in the sketches, and with each step I sense another possibility. This has worked out often enough—when I really have made a breakthrough—to give me encouragement to persevere in most cases. The final version of the School of Visual Arts retrospective poster, for instance, is much stronger than any of its preliminary stages. On the other hand, there are times when I move past the strongest moment, and the sketches are better

than the finish. I am trying more and more to accept my earlier versions of an illustration and to use them as finishes. Sometimes even a client finally chooses to use a sketch rather than a finish. This year [1981], a poster for the Art Institute of Pittsburgh—a case in which the client opted for the sketch rather than the finish—won a gold medal at the Society of Illustrators. So I should be encouraged by this to look a little harder at the first stages of my process. Actually, as I look back at a lot of work and the sketches that preceded it, I do see cases in which I needlessly pressed on.

MG: I wouldn't say it's needless. Your work is certainly characterized by more than one objective. There is a very romantic quality in your work as well as a great formalistic concern for the way pieces fit together and for the well-made object. And, of course, for me, those issues—which are sometimes contradictory and sometimes harmonious—are the richest and most central issues of art. One thing that characterizes your work and makes it unique is that all those contradictory concerns—the concern for self-expression, for the needs of the job, for the narrative, and for the formalistic relationships—all those questions and pieces and their resolution are what your work is about. This is what gives it its special quality.

Fort Wayne

1966
Westinghouse Broadcasting Co.
AD: Richard Nava

Westinghouse Broadcasting asked me to do a picture symbolizing Fort Wayne, Indiana. It was one of eight cities that they had similarly commissioned to different artists for a low-key advertising supplement in the Sunday *New York Times.* Their major radio stations were in these cities, and they wished to dramatize the size of their audience and the effectiveness of advertising on Westinghouse stations.

I went to Fort Wayne on a train that no longer exists, the *Broadway Limited,* and it seems to me that the experience of the train ride influenced what I did with the final picture as much as anything I later saw in Fort Wayne. I remember that it felt comfortable yet surreal to be on the train. Sitting inside my roomette watching the bleak October landscape, I became almost hypnotized by the telephone poles passing by in pulsating rhythm. I felt I was inside a perspective diagram—train tracks coverging to a point on the horizon. In my mind the telephone poles were marking the intervals of an invisible perspective grid. But it was not only space that was being measured; each pole was a marker in time, its disappearance past the window frame a moment lost forever. It was a melancholy idea. I tried to think about things that would prepare me for seeing Fort Wayne, but this childish anxiety took over my thoughts again until it seemed like a subject in itself. It was as though it had been revealed to me, as I was riding on this train, that to experience the long trip over the American heartland was to inevitably face the poignancy of time passing.

Later, in a light airplane belonging to the radio station manager, I again experienced the same feeling of melancholy. As we flew over the flat interlocking banners of Indiana farmland, the country seemed so enormous that I shrank down into my seat, overwhelmed by the notion that some chaotic force came out of this bigness that I would never be able to deal with. While I retreated into my topographical despair, the muscular station manager swung the plane in confident arcs, pointing out hives of industry or agriculture and shouting facts over the engine's roar.

The plane ride was only one of the ways I was shown Fort Wayne. Later that same day I was in a car being chauffeured through the expensive suburbs and then down the main street of town. At the end of this street was a large civic building, the Allen County courthouse, which was pointed out to me and described in terms of its architecture and age. Something about the way it was announced broke through my reverie. It was an important building in Fort Wayne. To my guides it was a unique object that people would want to take home with them as a postcard. I remember straining to see the building through the car window and to understand what made it different, but I couldn't keep it separate. In my mind it kept merging with a shifting hologram of pillars and cupolas which is my own stored postcard of every courthouse I have ever seen. There is some architectural ambivalence, I realized, in state buildings which are designed sufficiently alike to suggest that they all reflect part of the same majesty of the law, but which, at the same time, serve as specific local shrines.

These attempts to concentrate on the courthouse were strong enough, at least, to cut through the gloomy preoccupation I had felt since the train ride and began to get me focused on what I was seeing in Fort Wayne. My figurative awakening was just in time, as it happened. The next day I was taken on a tour of the factory where International Harvester trucks are assembled. It was the first time that I had ever seen a great industrial oper-

1

2

3

15

ation. It was to give me the central image for my painting and also the connecting idea for my reaction to the courthouse.

The truck factory was an immense space filled with different kinds of light. On the floor of the factory was a track with a beginning and an end and many logical manufacturing steps inbetween, but its simplicity was so hidden by the complex machinery for welding, riveting, shaping, fittings, and painting that its overall effect was that of a mechanical jungle. Following the track was fascinating, however, and it allowed me to see how the simple ladderlike frame becomes the rolling chassis with engine and, finally, the formidably filled-out truck. There was something particularly satisfying about the chassis and the way that the engine, as it sat nestled in its bare cradle, already emanated power and usefulness.

Back in New York I developed the single roll of film I had been moved to take, but it was the Fort Wayne postcards and the brochures from International Harvester that stimulated possibilities in my mind. I tried at first to take a more logical view of what I could say about Fort Wayne. In some of my first pencil doodles I toyed with straightforward images of the town as a major agricultural and industrial center. This impulse for an upbeat, all-American image got as far as a relatively finished painting. Actually, it was because of how I felt after I had done this picture—that its drama was impersonal and its information, visually boring—that convinced me to follow my less logical but more intuitive ideas. I faced the fact that I couldn't invent an authentic or interesting metaphor without using some of the strange reveries of the train ride. The three moments in my trip that had any real pungency for me were the fantasy of the perspective diagram and the mood that it provoked, my visual fascination with the truck chassis, and my reaction to the courthouse. In oblique ways they included several ideas important to Fort Wayne—the spaces of the Midwest, truck manufacture, and traditional values.

It struck me rather quickly that there was a natural connection between the first two things, that the chassis could be rolling along a perspective-diagram road, but I struggled awhile with integrating the courthouse. It was only after I had played around with the image of the trucks on a simplified landscape that I realized the idea of mass production could be applied to the courthouse too. In the actual painting I softened the idea, repeating the original building on the horizon on a series of postcards that probably bring to mind tourism more quickly than mass production. The postcards were a way to build a strong geometric shape in the sky that would echo the triangle of the road. I am still very satisfied by the tension between the curving wheels of the truck and the staccato corners of the postcards.

The drawing of the chassis is done in a relatively loose way, with many lines searching out the form. This character of revealed understructure in a drawing has always appealed to me. In this particular case, it is interesting that the "understructure" drawing is delineating an actual understructure.

Much about this painting is clumsy by my present standards—it is by far the oldest assignment I have included in this book. My immaturity in painting is very obvious in the heavy sky and the grayed color throughout, but for all that, it is still an important milestone for me. I learned something about using my moods, my real reactions, and even my resistance as raw materials for my art. I found out that given a choice, a picture is more powerful for being about authentic incidentals than unconvincing main events.

4

5

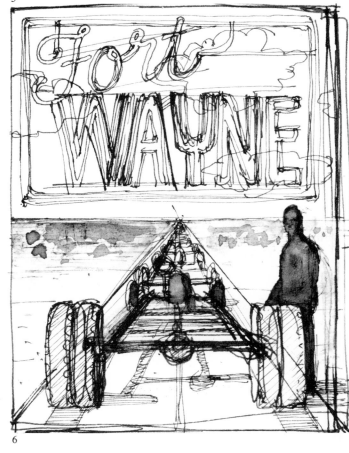

6

7

Portrait of My Future

January 17, 1972
New York magazine
AD: Milton Glaser

During the early 1970s, *New York* magazine offered in its pages a kind of layman's science of behavior. There were many articles dividing feelings and activities into categories that would, the writers claimed, help you direct your own life. Art director Milton Glaser invited me and two other artists, Ivan Chermayeff and Barbara Nessim, to illustrate one of these articles—"How to Get Control of Your Time (And Your Life)" by Jane O'Reilly. He asked us to think about our lives over the next twenty years—to ponder how we would use that time in relation to our art, to love, to money, to status . . . and then to express the result graphically. Milton gave each of us a full-color page in the magazine in which to express in a personal way how we felt about the future.

I took the assignment seriously, which made things very difficult. I did ponder my art, love, money, and status, but as all these things were in great transition or in chaos, it was very hard to anticipate the future. I had only recently accepted the fact that I had definitely made it into my thirties (I was thirty-seven), and in doing so had destroyed a cherished notion of my twenties: that I would die young. I was in the process of adjusting to a longer and different life, but nothing was clear enough to talk about.

As I tried to puzzle out a concept of my future, my own life—the piece of information I was asked to make sense of—seemed more and more confusing to me. So I stepped outside the information and suddenly realized that it was my impulse to tell the whole truth that was confusing me. The whole truth, if it were even available to me, was too complicated and probably boring. I had to "invent" this illustration as I would any other. Once I began to look at the details of my life as information to be selected and put together imaginatively, the picture took shape.

I began by thinking, what about my particular life would make the picture personal? I decided the most dramatic element would be my early years in China, where I was born. That period seemed to be a kind of launching pad for everything that was to follow. I chose to begin with a portrait of myself as a boy standing in the entrance to our house. The round gate and the beautiful curving trees that flanked it were interesting forms to paint. Next I decided to do away with all of the intermediate steps in my story and get right to the climax. I felt it was not necessary to symbolize the here-and-now me, since that was reflected in all the choices I was making with the picture.

The future, I was fairly sure, was going to be crazier; the central issue of my life would therefore be: how was I going to cope with this new lunatic world? Art would probably be the most stabilizing force in my life (and, in my mood of disobedience, it was the only issue I would deal with in this assignment), but I felt that its character would become not more chaotic, but more reflective and private. I symbolized this with a small pale tree being painted by a large brush. I enjoyed the fact that this suggested the idea of "return." The tree at the top not only echoed the Chinese trees at the bottom, but also its nature suggested an Eastern approach to painting. I framed my pale tree with a rectangle surrounded by tall, New Yorkish buildings twisting and turning in destructive frenzy.

Paradoxically, nine years later the picture seems as true as anything I might have said about myself or speculated about the future. New York did get crazier, my work has been a great comfort in my life, and it has become, if not always paler, at least purer in color and more personal. And I do paint with a big brush.

1   2

3

McMULLAN

Ages 16–22

February 1974
New York magazine
AD: Walter Bernard

1 | A magazine photo gave me information for the gasping boy's head.
2 | This photo of me jumping was the basis for the simplified body of the adolescent.
3 | These two magazine portraits had the severe expressions I wanted for the parents' faces.
4 | One of three color sketches I made to work out the subterranean mood.
5 | The finished painting.

In her book *Passages*, Gail Sheehy describes the difficult process of disentanglement young people must go through to leave their families and be on their own; she remarks that it typically takes three tries before the bond is cut. Something clicked in my mind when I read "three tries." Isn't that the same number of times we bob up out of the water when we are about to drown? Not only that, isn't the adolescent's impulse to leave the family like trying to find free air—to rid ourselves of the suffocation of parental love and rules and no privacy? Don't we sometimes feel we are drowning in the affection of our families?

A harsh symbol for leaving home, but in my picture—which would illustrate an excerpt from Sheehy's book in *New York* magazine—no one was really going to drown after all. Everyone would survive, including the strange parents living so comfortably in their clutter under the sea. I painted this scene with my mother's living room, and the claustrophobia it provoked in me, vividly in my mind. With a retrospective shudder, I summoned up a mental image of the tabletops in this room—every surface not occupied by small ivory figurines was covered with an interweaving of magazines, tortoiseshell cigarette boxes, tarnished silver ashtrays, nail polish and nail-polish remover, glasses with dregs of ginger ale or gin, glasses with cuttings of plants rooting themselves or dying. On the walls, ancient Chinese scroll paintings were jostled by strident chintz curtains. On the floors, several different carpets lapped up against each other like hostile tides sweeping in from other rooms. Add narrow shafts of sun squeezing between the drapes, and the room is complete.

Not much of this bric-a-brac actually got into the painting, of course, but these autobiographical feelings were really more important in helping me find the right metaphor and giving the illustration its comic sense of desperation (some people, I admit, find it more desperate than comic). Despite the claustrophobia, I particularly enjoyed painting the bottom part of the picture. The figures and the details of the room were painted over a basic sienna-to-purple background, which gave the scene a dense, subterranean quality. I tried to give the parents and their furniture an exaggerated quality, almost as though they were characters in a cartoon version of family life.

My feelings about space have had a great deal to do with the staging of my pictures in general. Along with not wanting to be surrounded by clutter, I am also not enthusiastic about the kind of person who edges closer and closer as he talks to me. I need more space than that. As you will notice in many of the images in this book, people are shown from head to toe as though the viewer has stepped back enough to see the entire scene. I like looking at an activity as though it were a tableau, and I strongly believe in observing the gestures of the body and using its expressiveness in my illustration. Knowing how a person's feet are placed, for instance, gives you an insight into the total attitude of the body. In this illustration, it was important that the adolescent's ascending body suggest escape. I found a picture of a leaping man which had the right character, and even though I simplified the information in the photo into a washy silhouette, I tried to catch the exact tilt of the feet and the spirit of the wrinkles in the trousers.

Perhaps the fact that it is a picture of me jumping is particularly appropriate; I was probably escaping a tide of porcelain figurines when the picture was taken.

1

2

3

4

Communication Arts Cover

May/June 1974
Coyne & Blanchard, Inc.
AD: Richard Coyne

1 | The first sketch, which I rejected as an uninteresting non sequitur.

2 | A favorite cut-glass tumbler.

3 | Because the streams of pouring whiskey in magazine liquor ads didn't have the right highlights, I took my own shot.

4 | This simple line sketch was all I needed before proceeding to the final art.

5 | The cover as it ran in June–July 1974.

At any given period of my working life, there are certain subjects or esthetic ideas that particularly interest me. These ideas, which run parallel to my actual assignments, have included visual elements such as maps and grids, one-point perspective, back views, and the shadows of flash photography. Often I use aspects of these ideas in my day-to-day work, but occasionally it is exciting to have an unrestricted assignment in which to really develop my private enthusiasms—as was the case when Richard Coyne of *Communication Arts* magazine asked me to do a cover. Of course, I wanted to do something that, however arbitrarily chosen as a subject, would look right once it was on the cover and would prepare the reader for the article on my work inside the magazine. Because the magazine's audience consists of fellow professionals, I felt some pressure to do a tour de force. I also wanted my image to mysteriously connect with the month of July, when the issue would reach the reader.

At that time I was interested in two subjects—flowers and a faceted drinking glass—that I had resurrected from my earliest art-class experience. Because they are the kind of still life objects likely to be put before beginning art students, I had for a long time thought of them as boring. Certainly the saccharine paintings of flowers produced by both the Sunday painter and the assembly-line commercial artist had not done much for the reputation of flowers as a subject. And I could remember the stiff, overworked renderings of glass jars I had done at some particularly anxious stage of my apprenticeship. However, in the same way we often rediscover, in our mid-thirties, a romantic composer that we had liked in our teens and rejected as corny in our twenties, I had become fascinated with painting flowers and a particular glass just because they *are* clichés.

My first sketch was an image of a wild rose springing from an unseen dune. Although it sits unexpectedly in front of a seascape, I had hoped that the austerity and strangeness of the setting would give the flower the impact of a talisman. I worked on this little picture for some time, enriching the basic watercolor with many layers of pastel, but despite all this effort I could not convince myself that my picture had transformed the flower into the mysterious object I had imagined. I kept the most successful element of my sketch, the seascape, and went on to see what I could do with my second object, the glass.

Perhaps a glass sitting in front of an ocean is no more logical than a flower, but from the first it felt right. I had only to do the barest linear sketch before I felt ready to embark on the finished painting. I think this "falling together" of the concept had a lot to do with my conviction about the glass, for it had strong associations from childhood. I remembered this sort of solid cut-glass tumbler from the dining tables in Calcutta and in Vancouver. I would turn the glass slowly on the white tablecloth and watch the simple vectors of light that radiated from its facets. When I look at the glass now, its light-bending properties are so straightforward, the simplicity of its cut arches so architectural, that it evokes for me everything that is reasonable and comforting about bourgeois English life.

The image of pouring water came to mind simply from playing with the idea of a glass and its contents, and from the fact that the picture already involved a huge body of water. It was interesting to juxtapose one idea of water with another.

The cover came out in July, and I thought it looked like a vision you might see as you lie on the sand on a very hot day, when everything is clear, almost soundless, and not quite connected.

1

2

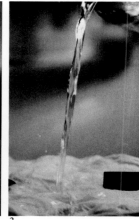

3

4

Vol. 16, No. 2 · $3

COMMUNICATION ARTS

Big Apple Poster

Summer 1974
School of Visual Arts
AD: Silas Rhodes

1 | A precursor to the Big Apple poster, this imaginary map of Long Island appeared in a potato cookbook.
2 | The color sketch.
3 | The finished poster.

I have always been fascinated by maps, not so much for their use to me in figuring out how to get from here to there, but simply for their beauty. I enjoy decoding a map's fussiness—letting my focus drop through successive webs of information till I finally reach the most delicate demarcations and the tiniest letters and numbers. I see a map as a complex and abstract picture in which sensuous coastlines and eccentric pools of slightly varying color are set against the severe geometry of a grid. It makes me think of the world of dreams, and of chaotic forces struggling against the fences and orderliness of the daytime world.

I have used this complex texture of maps in many of my assignments, sometimes as a ghostly, diagrammatic backdrop for nongeographic information and sometimes turning the idea itself into a map. The first time I made this transmutation, I did a map of Long Island in which the island became a potato. The illustration was for a potato recipe book edited by Myrna Davis, and my art was a play on the fact that Long Island is a center for potato growing on the East Coast. I carefully drew the map in pencil, giving the potato's surface an intricate scaliness that I hoped might also read as tiny roads and towns.

My second map concept was for a School of Visual Arts poster. Silas Rhodes, the head of the school, asked me to design a poster for the school using the headline "Spend a few nights with us. It may change the way you spend the rest of your days." The poster was to be one of a series displayed in the subways of New York to promote the school. It did not immediately occur to me to convey the headline with a Big Apple map, but after toying with concepts that had to do with night, day, and art school, I began a train of thought that led to the final poster.

The first step of this process was thinking about the fantasy that the headline implicitly tugged at: the dream of fame and fortune in the world of graphic art. I then reasoned that since most reputations, and occasionally fortunes, are made in the marketplace of Manhattan, the city represents an Eldorado of the arts. Now, if I could just show the city in such a way that it would symbolize this pinnacle of achievement, I would have an image for the poster that would illuminate the headline's meaning. It was at this point that I remembered the name that jazz musicians of the twenties used to describe Manhattan's being at the top—the Big Apple. It was a short jump to thinking of a map in which a juicy red apple replaces the isle of Manhattan. Once I had worked out how the shapes of the other boroughs bend around the apple and how the hot red of the apple leaps across the water and begins to suffuse the other land masses, I thought of a way to make the image spatial and give the idea of the map some surprising variation. This was achieved by painting the water at the bottom so that it seems to bend away from its flat, two-dimensional shape and move toward the viewer as a series of waves existing in perspective.

Because of the large, simple shapes of this poster, the watercolor could be exploited for all of its flowing, color-merging qualities. Also, because this was one of the first times that the reproduction of my work was going to be dramatically bigger than the original, I had a chance to see how the gesture of my painting blew up. Not bad.

It is hard to imagine now, given the current resurgence of the nickname's popularity, but at the time of the poster's publication, there were a number of people who were confused by my metaphor and asked me why I had made Manhattan into a big apple. A better question might have been, why did I forget to identify Brooklyn? but I have no good answer to it.

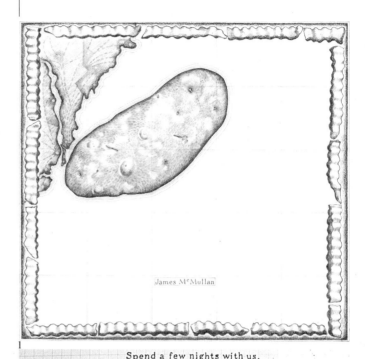

1

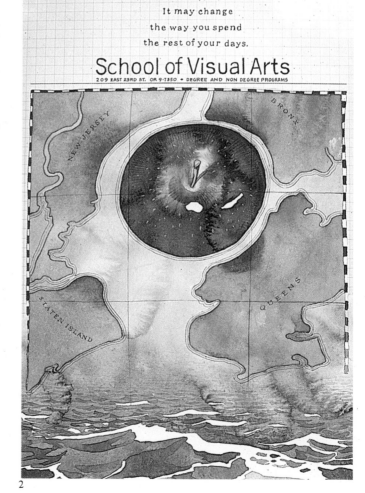

Spend a few nights with us.
It may change
the way you spend
the rest of your days.

School of Visual Arts
209 EAST 23RD ST. OR 9-7350 • DEGREE AND NON DEGREE PROGRAMS

2

School of Visual Arts

209 East 23rd Street, New York, N.Y. 10010 · 679-7350

Spend a few nights with us.
It may change the way you spend
the rest of your days.

**Degree and Non-Degree Programs. Film, Photography, Media Arts (Advertising, Fashion, Illustration, Design)
Fine Arts (Painting, Sculpture, Printmaking, Crafts), Video Tape, Dance.**

Rain

1975
Sesame Street magazine
AD: Henry Wolf

The magazine *Sesame Street* was developed in the early seventies as a print adjunct to the history-changing television program by the same name. For most of its publishing life the magazine has faithfully reflected its electronic mentor, presenting its educational message with the same graphics and cartoon characters one sees on the TV program. Big Bird and Cookie Monster have been as ever present on the pages of the magazine as on the TV screen.

From 1974 to 1976, however, when the magazine was art directed by Henry Wolf, it had a more independent life as a publication. The visual means it used for getting across information on reading, numbers, and logic were quite different from those of the television program. During this period it was often difficult to find even one Big Bird in the pages of *Sesame Street.*

As an artist, Henry Wolf instinctively realized how boring it is to make a picture using someone else's cartoon character. If there is such a thing as a graphic-art purgatory, it is probably a place where artists have to illustrate the Divine Comedy using Big Bird and Ernie as the principal characters. At any rate, Henry assigned the various magazine pieces to illustrators as independent problems that did not have to reflect the TV program. He only asked that the images be to the point and beautiful. What he got were some extraordinary pages of art for which the magazine won many awards.

One of the jobs I did for *Sesame Street* magazine during this period was on the subject of rain. The assignment was typical—a presentation of a simple subject, through a few of its aspects, that could be used as a starting point for discussion between a parent or teacher and a child. I was given a list of possible ways of illustrating rain, among them puddles, rainbows, animals drinking, flowers growing, and so on.

The subject rang a "Christopher Robin" bell with me, and I visualized a kid playing around in the rain with an umbrella. I didn't have a child available to model for me on the next rainy day, and so I took my petite young assistant out on the street and began photographing different kinds of poses. When we came up with the arrangement of the tilted umbrella reflected in a puddle, I knew I had my basic picture. The information in the reflection was wonderful. It was the kind of thing you had to see in reality in order to know how to depict it. I was also delighted with the fact that the whole thing came out of a very urban situation. It is easy to make a lyrical picture about the middle of a woods, but more interesting to make one about the decaying sidewalks of New York.

My work on *Sesame Street* changed my mind about dealing with children's material. In my early years as an illustrator I had had some disastrous encounters with children's books. In my illustrations for two of these books, I had agonizingly tried to match the sweetness of the words. I followed these debacles by trying to use collage to disguise my inherent lack of whimsy. Finally, and only after the *New York Herald Tribune* had called my collage book "the most uncomfortable art of the season," I swore never to darken the nursery door again. What I learned working for *Sesame Street* was that if I limited myself to simple visual explanations, I could make pictures that children would enjoy. In truth, once I began to do these pictures enthusiastically, I'm not sure I was really conscious of what made them different from adult illustrations.

1

2

3

James McMullan

4

Scholastic Posters

1976–1980
Let's Find Out magazine, Scholastic Publishing
AD: Carol Carson

The group of posters (eight in all) that I did for the Scholastic publication *Let's Find Out* stands somewhat apart from the rest of my work. Five of them are essentially nature posters with no human figures, and this makes them, in the most obvious sense, different from many of my other illustrations. For me, the experience of making landscape paintings, with all the inherent opportunity for abstraction and the designing of big forms, is a kind of holiday from the more rigorous demands of drawing and painting the figure. This esthetic freedom, along with the fact that the posters are meant to convey very simple, uncomplicated facts to their young audience, give the works a lyrical good-naturedness not typical of all my illustration. I must add that my relationship with Carol Carson, the art director, and Jean Marzollo, the editor, provided the best possible context for doing happy work. They originally came to me with great enthusiasm for the paintings I had done for *Sesame Street* magazine, and they gave me real freedom in finding ways to visually communicate their teaching objectives in the posters. Because so much excellent work was done during Carol's art directorship of *Let's Find Out*, I am sure I was not the only artist to find it an especially congenial situation.

One of the ways in which Carol and Jean were particularly sympathetic to my point of view was in their willingness to let me stage the information in the posters more realistically than is often done in artwork for the magazine's age group. I am not comfortable with "storybook" space, for instance, in which objects and people are shown much larger than they would actually be in relation to their background and the plane on which they stand tends to be tilted upward.

In the Barnyard Game poster, I show the farm animals in a realistic relationship to each other and to the farm buildings by using an aerial view of the whole landscape. I knew that this is a sophisticated point of view for first graders, but I trusted in the crispness of my painting and the attractive patterning to make the poster understandable and interesting. The large scale of these posters, 22″ x 32″ (56 x 81 cm), created an unusual opportunity in itself, and in the Barnyard Game, as with each of the others, I tried to use an idea that would take advantage of this relatively luxurious space.

In the Prairie Animals poster, I wanted to create a panoramic feeling. I also had to show the animals up close, which I decided to do by painting enlarged details in circles (very much like the call-outs often used in diagrams), which floated in the sky and were joined to appropriate points in the landscape by thin lines. Conceiving this, as well as many of my other ideas for the Scholastic posters, was not difficult; it was like moving toward an inevitable and natural solution. The difficult part of this poster was the research for the prairie vegetation, but as is so often the case for me, the difficulty engendered the best part of the painting.

I could not find good pictures of a broad expanse of flat prairie. Early photographs of the right kind of terrain are often indistinct, and many contemporary pictures I found were romantic shots of lush, flowering prairie that didn't fit my own idea of what the "wild" prairie looks like. I had imagined some kind of rough grass, but in my earlier attempts to actually get at the texture of blades of grass, I had made a terrible, dense mess of it. This time I began by laying in large, light washes of color that established horizontal planes moving progressively back into the picture, dotted by small "rosettes" of low bushes. Then I began to paint an abstract pattern of grass, which I visualized more as

1

2

3

4

28

5

6

Scholastic Posters

the spaces between intersecting blades of grass than the grass itself. Using the natural shapes of the brush strokes and keeping in mind the idea of the openings between the blades of grass, I carefully built up a texture which became finer as it moved up the picture plane. I added daubs of brighter color to represent the blades of grass, but I really continued to think of the painting more as a tapestry than a representation of actual grass. The entire thing was an invention, perhaps one of the most abstract pieces of painting I had done up to that point, and it was very evocative and satisfying for me.

About a year after I finished the Prairie Animals poster, Carol Carson commissioned me to do two more posters for the series, showing a salt marsh in the fall and in the spring. Fortunately, at that time I was working at my house in Sag Harbor, which looks out on a cove with many of the characteristics of a salt marsh. The edge of the cove is ringed with dark green marsh grass and tall reeds, and many marsh birds such as egrets and some occasional herons feed in the grasses or fly by. Although I needed to show the particular conformation of a salt marsh that exists directly behind the dunes of the open ocean, the character of the view from my studio did have a great deal to do with the colors and the light of the finished painting. There is an egret that frequents the water's edge near our house, and I remember watching him fly by on many evenings, his wings almost touching the water. I included this bird in my painting of the salt marsh in the fall.

In the salt marsh posters, like the two before them, I needed to show animals close up as well as within the landscape. For these posters I thought of a variation of the circular call-outs I had used in the prairie painting; this time, I enclosed the detailed animals in eccentrically shaped bubbles that connected to their position in the landscape with a series of ever smaller descending bubbles, a device often used to indicate characters' thoughts in cartoons. Maybe the marsh itself was thinking up the animals— or perhaps the animals were being elevated in bubbles of marsh gas. Although in a different situation an editor or art director might have objected to the lack of strict logic in the bubble idea, both Jean Marzollo and Carol Carson saw that the bubbles looked right and that they got across the information about the animals and where they lived in the marsh.

There is also an arbitrary element in the last of the posters I have included here, the Train Game. The bridge is a gratuitous addition, in the sense that it has nothing to do with the information I was asked to convey about the train and what it carries. But, as you can see, it was a powerful element for me in organizing the design of the poster and dramatizing the train itself. Because I was working on a large scale, I could make the train relatively small and depend on the precision of my painting to carry the details of the different cars. The bridge, with the tension of height and the potential fall it implies, gives the flat side view of the train an excitement it would not have otherwise. It evokes for me those suspenseful movie scenes where the train may or may not make it across the secretly damaged bridge. If you compare my original sketch with the finished piece, you will notice that the construction of the bridge is more delicate and airy in the sketch. In retrospect, I see that I should have kept the struts just as delicate in the final painting. I am satisfied, however, with the juicy greens of the mountain slopes and the suggestion of misty space beyond the ravine.

8

9

10

11

12

Scholastic Posters

13

14

15

Comedians

1976 Broadway play
Producer: Alexander H. Cohen

The only time I am ever sure I am being really funny in a drawing is when I toss off a quick birthday, anniversary, or general celebration card for my wife, Katy. Usually these are watercolor cartoons depicting some absurd aspect of our domestic life in which, more often than not, I represent myself as an inept but lovable, half-crazy balding man. On occasion I have tried to get some of this quick, manic spirit into an assignment, but the humor never quite survives the transplantation. Either the kind of ideas I use in Katy's cards are not really that funny when used out of context or else, like Woody Allen, I can't make a joke without myself as the fall guy. I suspect too that when I make a picture for a client I "perfect" the technique and in doing so destroy the comic spontaneity of the wilder private cards.

What I often end up with in ostensibly funny assignments is a "ha-ha" quality that has a curious edge to it, like a nervous laugh that somewhat undercuts the intended good humor. This quality, however, was perfectly suited to the spirit of a play called *Comedians*, for which I did the poster.

This essentially sardonic play by the British author Trevor Griffiths uses its setting, a night school for comedians, as a way of dealing with the shallowness of contemporary life and the bitterness of the English class struggle. The play starts in a naturalistic style with some very funny joke-telling but becomes progressively surreal and angry in its tone. I thought it was a powerful and ambitious play that deserved a longer run than its eight weeks in New York. It was produced by Alexander Cohen and directed by Mike Nichols, who was, through a chain of events, responsible for my getting involved.

Mike Nichols had just directed the play *Streamers* for Joseph Papp, and as for all Papp productions at that time, Paul Davis had done the poster, a marvelous image of a man falling through the air. Nichols was understandably impressed with Paul's work, and when he agreed to direct *Comedians* for Alexander Cohen, he asked Paul to do the poster. Paul had to decline because he had an exclusive agreement to do only Joseph Papp's posters, but he was kind enough to recommend me to Nichols. This assignment made possible my debut into designing theatrical posters. I like to tell this part of the story because it is so illuminating. Interesting contacts in this business often are made, not as you might expect—from being in shows, winning awards, or frequently having one's work in the media—but from some almost accidental crossing of paths, as it did in my case. This poster has led to a continuing professional relationship with Cohen and to my doing five other theatrical posters to date. I was fortunate that this connection happened at a time when Paul Davis, through his series of posters for Papp, had raised everyone's consciousness about how good posters can be.

When I took the assignment, I was given the script of the play with no particular instructions. When I read the play, I liked its seriousness and complexity. It seemed to me a very daring notion to take humor and turn it back on itself in the way that Griffiths did. My first idea, the comedian whose nonexistent head is replaced by a speech bubble containing the name of the play, tried to express how the comedians in the play used or abused their identities in their desperate need to be funny. I hoped that the art might suggest more than this, really—perhaps even a larger mood of existential desperation.

It was just this seriousness that got my sketch into serious trouble with Cohen and Nichols. As Nichols said in summing up his objections and exhorting me on to another try, "I want a poster from you which is appealing enough to get the people into the theater. We'll let them know about the hard parts later." The sketch was simply too glum and perhaps too static. Looking back now, I think I had designed it too much like a book jacket, seeing the idea in terms of a scale that was both physically and symbolically too small and restrained.

Actually, two very helpful things happened at this point. One was a long phone conversation with Mike Nichols in which he explained his view of the play, and the other was my being provided with a set of English production photographs. I will digress here for a moment to comment on reference pictures and clients. Perhaps because clients think that an artist's imagination will work with a more grandiose sweep unfettered by details, many clients withhold (or at least forget about) photographic or other kinds of reference materials they may have; typically, this usually indispensable picture research does not come to light until some crisis in the job provokes the client to remember it. I try to impress upon the people I work with that I do not really invent from thin air but from my responses to real physical information and that if they have wonderful (or awful) pictures of their subject hidden in a drawer, I really need to see them. Often, as in the case of *Comedians*, the client has pictures that I would have no other way of getting, pictures that often contain unique and surprising information. The pictures of the English production of *Comedians* opened up a whole gamut of gestures and costume and lighting that was like a treasure chest to me at that point. In them, I could see first-rate actors expressing the ideas of the play in body language that I don't think I ever could have imagined or directed my own models to do. As you will see, one of these photographs became the basis for the poster's main image.

To get back to the conversation with Mike Nichols: he spoke at some length on his view that a poster should be a simple and dramatic image. But more important to me, he described which aspects of the play he felt could be used in a poster to symbolize the whole work—the cheap, aggressive quality of the nightclub comedians represented in the play. Although no real image had been decided upon, I came away from this conversation with an understanding of Mike Nichols's central ideas about this play.

I began looking at the photographs from Alexander Cohen. They were mostly from the second act of the play, in which the student comedians are perfecting their routines in a working-class club. I used as my starting point photographs of a bespectacled comedian in a ruffled shirt and tuxedo who gestures aggressively with his hand. I was intrigued by the way in which the shadow of his glasses on the planes of his cheeks underlined the quality of theatrical spotlighting. The image had the virtue of quick readability, but after doing three pencil sketches, I became bored with its simplicity. As is often the case with me, I felt uncomfortable basing my design on only the effect of the head and hands—it was cropped too closely for me.

It was at this point that I began working with the photograph of actor Jonathan Pryce doubled over laughing. It is a strange and eccentric picture showing Pryce's figure midway in a complicated gesture. Often, when a pose like this is frozen by the speed of the camera, it is too idiosyncratic to make any sense, but in this case I was attracted to its odd rhythm and tense angularity. To me the comedian's figure seemed to suggest he had been laughing so hard and so long that his laughter had become hysterical. At first I simply saw him laughing, and then I wondered if he was laughing about something really funny. Since humor is

1,2 | Two pencil variations on the speech
      bubble idea.
  3 | Unused color sketch in which the
      background overwhelms the figure.

1

2

3

Comedians

used in this play to express anger against the English establishment, I decided this pose was an entirely appropriate image for the poster.

I realized that the figure in my poster must be read quickly as a cliché comedian, and so I replaced Jonathan Pryce's casual outfit with evening clothes and substituted longer hair for Pryce's punkish crop. In my first color sketch, I gave him a white dinner jacket, pink pants, and a "Skeezix" shock of blondish hair. The effect was disappointing, not simply because the color didn't unify the design but because my approach to the image was so prosaic. The brown drawing lines I used looked plodding and uninspired to me; I had found the right thing to draw, but not the magical way to draw it. After thinking about my problem for a while, a strange but useful association came to mind; the figure reminded me of a stork. Suddenly I saw it elongated and balanced precariously on one stiltlike leg. In the pencil sketch you can see my visualization of this stork man: not only has the leg grown, but also the shapes have become spikier and more birdlike. Also, the lettering has moved from its boring position at the top of the poster into a series of arcs that accentuate the jabbing motion of the head. I decided that the importance of the figure's silhouette dictated a more calligraphic approach to the painting. Instead of drawing the figure in a linear way, I would use a brush to draw the whole shape as a series of large strokes, just as one might write a Chinese character. This also led me to paint the figure essentially in one color and to make the suit simply a variation of the blue background. The whole design was beginning to pull together for me, and I plunged ahead to do the sketch I would show to Nichols and Cohen.

My sketch turned out so well that not only did the two men approve it, but also Cohen wanted to go ahead and use it as the finish. I told him I wanted to do another version to improve the clarity of the color and make the comedian's face sharper and clearer in tone. Had I stuck to my word and simply made those changes, I would have avoided a great deal of trouble. I decided, however, to make the experience of doing the finish more interesting for myself by adding another, "improving" element. I attempted to add theatrical back lighting to the man's figure as though blue spotlights were shining on him from the wings. This new element required a new suit color—I used purplish maroon—and a more premeditated approach to the painting because, instead of using large brushstrokes to describe the figure, I had to paint carefully around the shapes that would contain the blue highlights. Given enough time, perhaps I might have invented a good way to include the highlights, but the painting I actually did was stiff and totally lacked the spirit of the sketch. But, in the flush of having just done it, I was blind to its shortcomings. At that moment, I thought it looked richer and more perfect than the sketch.

To Cohen and Nichols the poster looked wrong. With no hesitation, they both said they preferred the sketch, and after emotionally but unsuccessfully defending it, I returned to my studio with the false finish under my arm. Following a good night's sleep, I looked again and saw my mistake, and I had to face the difficulty of redoing the image from my sketch without losing any of its spontaneity. Happily, when I became involved with the actual painting, the challenge of making the color clearer and the washes more flowing kept me alert and interested. I think my final watercolor did, in the end, embody all the lively, calligraphic qualities and color I had hoped for.

4

5

6

7

8

9

10 | The sketch that was approved by the producer and director.

11 | The "false finish." Adding blue highlights to the figure turned out to be a mistake, and the poster was rejected by the client.

12 | A loosening up exercise I did just before starting the final painting.

13 | The final version.

10

11

12

Spring Training

March 7, 1977
Sports Illustrated
AD: Richard Gangel

In New York I am known as an artist who does theatrical posters, illustrations of ironic subjects for *Esquire* and *New York* magazine, record jackets, and other arcane items such as posters for the School of Visual Arts. When I am teaching at a school outside the city or speaking to one of the art directors' clubs across the country, I notice that people have a different idea of the kind of work I do. In America at large it seems I am known for my work in *Sports Illustrated.* It makes sense, of course, because *Sports Illustrated* is the most widely read national magazine for which I regularly illustrate.

Apart from my pique at not being appreciated outside of New York for the full range of my oeuvre, I have another problem with my reputation as a sports artist: a great many people in places like Kansas City or Seattle expect me to be able to talk about sports! While I am quite prepared to talk about how the shadow of a stadium creates a dark monster that finally devours the afternoon game, or to speculate on the real reasons baseball players chew gum, I know nothing about runs, hits, or errors. It is with a certain fascinated disbelief that I listen to someone identify the uniforms and thus the teams in one of my illustrations. My God, did I really leave the colors sufficiently alone to represent the uniforms of a real team?

Aside from my middling game in tennis, I have never been an athlete. I went to the kind of English-style schools where a great deal of time and brutality was used to make young men good at sports, but I resisted all this to the end. Despite my school experiences, I have always harbored an admiration for athletes. They are courageous, physically beautiful, and able to use their bodies in a high sphere of activity that seems to transcend effort. Sometimes a champion diver, for instance, seems magically supported by joy rather than technique. I can identify with that level of accomplishment, for I too have rare moments when my creative involvement takes me to a higher plane than I could reach with hard work alone. I like to watch certain sports, but I see them almost abstractly. It is hard for me to feel the importance of one side or the other winning. The players' faces and personalities have interest for me only as momentary sparks in the ebb and flow of the game's pattern.

In painting sports subjects, I don't think I am limited by not being an athlete or a true sports fan. I am a watcher, and although what I watch is often not what I am meant to watch, I think there is some good in that. With sophisticated television cameras and telephoto lenses, certainly nobody needs me to capture the best plays of the game.

These are the attitudes with which I embarked on my assignment to cover spring training at the Cleveland Indians' camp in Tucson, Arizona. Richard Gangel, the art director for *Sports Illustrated,* had no illusions about my knowledge of baseball, but apparently he had no reservations about sending me either.

At the training camp in Tucson, I was very much on my own. There were no other journalists around, and in the early part of the day, there were very few spectators in the stands. The team came out of the locker room gate and began to run around the field in a large, informal group, joking and calling to each other as they ran. I wandered around the middle of the field, taking occasional photographs of the runners and of the advertisements that were painted on the fence. After a while the players stopped running and formed more or less regular ranks to do stationary exercises. No one spoke to me directly, but as I started to photograph them in their straining, contorted positions, their jokes seemed as much for my benefit as their own. I don't think they were used to being observed in this aspect of their training, and they were probably a little uncomfortable about it. As I began to get involved in the possibilities of what I was seeing, I too started moving faster and taking some fairly odd positions in order to get the shots. I used a medium telephoto lens (which I don't ordinarily like) to photograph from a distance, which I hoped would alleviate the self-consciousness all around. I had a hunch that what I was seeing might be as interesting as anything I would see on the trip, and so I took a lot of shots.

I was impressed with the seriousness of the exercises. In their difficult stretching routines, many of the players were exhibiting a litheness I would have expected more from gymnasts than from baseball players. (My conception of baseball players, it is true, has been forever marked by seeing pictures of the thick-waisted Babe Ruth.) The players I was seeing in Tucson were so young, limber, and good-looking that they might have been the cast of a baseball movie.

The entire scene had the quality of being almost too perfect to be true. The stadium was clean, well designed, and newly painted with an artificial but totally optimistic turquoise blue. The grounds were neat and well cared for, and the grass was persistently green. The players were friendly and, at least on the surface, radiated the confidence that came from knowing they were among the Ricks and Dereks that had made it through the whole damn pro machine to the top.

These young men had spent most of their lives preparing for the big leagues and, understandably, they expected anyone on assignment from *Sports Illustrated* to know a great deal about the sport. What does one talk about with a twenty-two-year-old pro ballplayer except baseball? I realized then that my lack of knowledge about baseball seriously limited my effectiveness as a journalist. It was like being in Paris and not being able to speak French. It was even difficult to explain my purpose in being there—that I was taking photos in order to turn them into paintings. I could see the question "Why?" in their faces. The ballplayers were used to looking at their exact photographic likenesses in the pages of sports magazines: why, then, would I want to interfere with this lovely arrangement?

But interfere with it I did. In my sketches of the exercise photos, for instance, it was the intricacy of the body movements that interested me—not the details that would have identified particular players. In my view of spring training I never seriously considered showing the players in the heroic moments of the game. Instead I focused on the odd, off-center images such as the exercises and the pre-game warm-ups—or at the other extreme, the lethargic, suspended moments one experiences while watching the panorama of a practice game from the almost empty stands on a sunny day. The pictures I got have a feeling of distance and timelessness that I somehow distilled from an experience that had many other facets. I think my images are an accurate reflection of the separateness I felt at the time, as well as my desire to make something out of what I *could* understand about spring training.

There were other things I remember about my time in Tucson that didn't work for me in the illustrations. One was the camaraderie of the players. I could sense how glad they were to be doing what they were doing and how special the understanding was between them—only the other players could really know and share what it all meant. I also remember the curious theatricality

1 | An idea for using geometric lines over the exercising players.
2 | One of the sketches from my first conception of the assignment.
3, 4 | Photographs I took in Tucson.
5 | A sketch derived from photo 4.

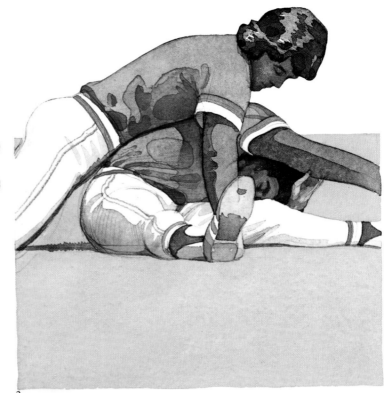

1

2

3

4

5

of the beginning of the well-attended exhibition games at night, when the glow of dusk was suddenly superceded by the orangy blast of field lights. The light gave everything a Halloweenlike quality, and crazy pale shadows crisscrossed over faces lit from a dozen different directions. There was a carnival mood in the stadium, too, with kids and sometimes young women hanging over the concrete lip of the dugout roof, dangling heads and arms and programs trying to get the attention of the players by repeating their names over and over. The players in the dugout sat staring straight ahead or talked among themselves as though this fringe of faces did not exist. I remember, too, the elderly retired men who would sit in the stands during the day to watch the field practice. They had sat in these same stands for years, and when they spoke of the players you might have thought they were talking about their grandsons or old friends. Sometimes one of them would call out as a player passed near the stands and the player would answer, using the man's name. They *were* old friends.

Perhaps the ideal way to do paintings or stories about spring training is to have enough time and patience to watch from the stands like the old men, season after season. I know that when I got back to New York and began to sort through my photographs, I spent a long time thinking and sketching before I began to see what I had looked at and to know what I thought. In fact, the first series of sketches I did met with bemused puzzlement from art director Dick Gangel. In them I had tried to distill the players' stretching exercises down to close-up images of entangled limbs. I had hoped to achieve something provocative in this way, but Dick's lack of enthusiasm encouraged me to think again. All he would tell me at that point was that he thought of spring training as a beginning. I realized I had cogitated so much about the trip and what I had seen that my sketches had become convoluted and hermetic. I was trying too hard to see spring training from an entirely unique perspective.

I started a new series of sketches, this time concentrating on the mechanics of the exercises. How could I suggest their movement and also the discipline involved? I did a few sketches in which curved, diagrammatic lines overlaid the images of the athletes to describe the trajectories of their motions. Nice try, but no go. I then tried showing the players distributed over the grass in a naturalistic perspective. The simplicity of the arrangement was an improvement, but the perspective didn't do much to convey a sense of the mechanics. Then it occurred to me to use my old friend, the grid, and to show one exercise per grid box. The layout resembled that of a primer of some sort, or even a technical manual. I liked it. The one problem that remained was the grass. The color green has always given me trouble. I can't seem to combine yellowish grassy hues well with other colors, and I abhor green in its olive incarnations. Basic Hooker's green has the technical drawback of being one of the few watercolors that tends to stain the paper immediately, creating an unintended hard edge that can't be softened. For this assignment, I thought about grass, looked at its real color, and decided that I could do better than that. I mixed up my own version of grass color—a beautiful, creamy, blue-tinged green that was a mixture of at least six colors. My painting of the exercises depended a great deal for effect on the posterlike surface created by the even washes of this new green flowing around the simply described figures. The whites of the uniforms were dramatically isolated in this design, and I took a great deal of pleasure in laying-in very light purplish blue tones to describe the forms of the white sec-

6

7

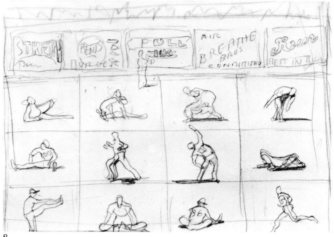
8

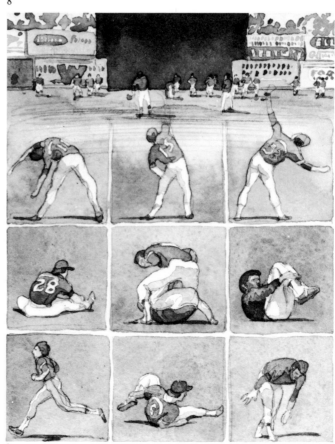
9

11, 12 | Two color sketches in which I experimented with slightly different approaches to painting the spectators.

13 | The finished spectator painting.

tions without losing their brilliance. In doing this painting, I moved ahead one or two notches in my ability to utilize the luminous qualities of very light washes.

My second painting was about the spectators and what they were watching. Because in this case I was more interested in showing the people in the stands than the players, I decided to use a surrealistic change of scale to increase the size of the watchers in relation to the players. This is not an unusual trick, but I liked the way the horizontals of the big bleachers merged into the architecture of the small-scale scene. When it ran in the magazine, this picture provoked a woman to write to me, saying she had recognized her father, who was retired in Florida and never missed a day at the stadium watching spring training. The man she was so convinced of is the shadowy little figure in the red hat, second from the left. My suggestive way with simple washes was much more effective than I had thought—not only could I summon up her father with a little blob of Winsor & Newton, but I could also transport him from Florida to Arizona.

It would be wrong for me to suggest that, after my struggle with the first painting, I moved confidently and smoothly through the rest. I did many small sketches I never used; I abandoned paintings, and I also completed more paintings than the magazine could print. There were several photographs of ballplayers relaxing that had the spirit of comradeship I liked, but they didn't have enough narrative drama. It was also difficult for me to stick to one conceptual point of view—the exercises struck me as diagrammatic, the spectators seemed surreal, and the subject of my last painting, a young player leaning on a fence watching the beginning of a game, I saw as a romantic image of hope and springtime. (Maybe in this one I had finally dealt with Richard Gangel's idea of spring training as a beginning.)

My experiences in going to Tucson and doing these paintings led me to believe that it is much better to know something about your subject than to depend entirely on your visual and intellectual reflexes, as I had done with this assignment. Another time, I would like to be able to ask intelligent questions and to feel appropriate wonder about the people I am watching. Besides patience, this kind of work depends on the knack of "hanging out," which is knowing when to make the right noises and when to be silent. I am fascinated with Michael Herr's book, *Dispatches*, which deals with the relationship of a journalist and his subjects. Herr brilliantly reveals the complexity of what it feels like to be the watcher and also to become part of the chemistry of what is being watched. I like to believe there are several styles of journalism that will work in a situation. I don't have much taste for the method I see most often, that of "plunging in," where the journalist quickly and aggressively establishes his presence in the middle of the activity and then works out from this beachhead in wider and wider arcs. My style is more of a circling one; I move quietly around the perimeter of activity and then slowly and carefully into the center. When this works, I have the advantage of picking up nuances that might be otherwise overlooked.

Aside from the few examples such as Ralph Steadman, Felix Topolski, and Bill Maulden in our time, and scattered historical figures such as George Catlin and Winslow Homer, there is not a strong tradition for artists acting as independent journalists or even as equal partners with writers. For the most part, editors have seen illustrations as naturally following words, yet I think there are rich, unexplored possibilities in the idea of artists choosing a journalistic subject and pursuing it independently. In

11

12

13

most cases some words are necessary in order for the pictures to exist comfortably within the magazine format as we know it, but there is no reason why an artist intelligent enough to organize a pictorial essay couldn't provide a good text. Steadman does it beautifully, and Ed Sorel, although not exactly an on-the-scene journalist, is able to write and to generate contexts for his drawings. Richard Gangel has single-handedly promoted this journalistic aspect of art for years by sending artists out to cover events like spring training and the Kentucky Derby. Many of the results have been good or at least interesting, but Gangel is bucking the fact that most illustrators generally lack experience in thinking and working in this way. If other magazines besides *Sports Illustrated* gave journalistic assignments, illustrators would have more opportunities to learn the skill. Besides, it is really more than just a technique that has to be learned. It would take a big change in attitude for most illustrators to believe they could develop stories based on their own observations, and opinions.

A journalistic approach to illustration could still develop, if for no other reason than the change that has occurred in magazines themselves. They have become more passive, operating on the essentially reactive marketing theories that are now so endemic. Besides the pragmatic creation of special-interest magazines to cover topics such as running or real estate, there is an increasing shift in editorial policy toward watching reader surveys and responding automatically to "hot" topics. It seems to me that the days of the magazine reflecting one person's vision are almost over (or at least until the next eccentric, rich editor/publisher creates such a magazine that can make money). The importance of the particular writer's voice or point of view has been replaced largely by the idea of the writer-artisan who can write well on any subject. Magazines are not likely to buy a powerful, personal piece of journalism unless they can see it as a finished work that the writer or artist has produced independently.

If illustrators are to continue to do interesting, personal work, I think they will have to abandon the notion of the magazine as a paternalistic, nurturing institution that supports the developing talent of an illustrator in the way that the *Saturday Evening Post* supported Norman Rockwell. Illustrators must replace this relationship with a more independent and entrepreneurial one, creating contexts for their work by thinking of ideas, writing their own material, or teaming up with writers to do projects.

I realize that what I am proposing would mean an enormous change in the thinking and working habits of the illustrator. It would involve a financial restructuring of the free-lancer's life so that he or she could keep going economically while working on independent projects. It also would mean selling topics to editors whose view of the world is narrowly focused on "hit parade" subjects and "hard news." Learning to work independently and initiate projects is definitely a drastic change for illustrators who have been used to concentrating on their craft and letting their clients worry about the whys and whens of their assignments. The alternative to making such a change is for artists to accept increasingly predesigned assignments and a diminished creative role in magazines. It is inevitable that editors will manipulate the contents of magazines more and more to conform to market-researched ideas of what "the product" should be. While the future promises restricted creativity and diminishing fees for the magazine illustrator, it also offers the freedom to act and to change, since there is so very little to lose. Perhaps we should be starting our own magazines.

14

15

16

17

18

Brooklyn Disco

June 7, 1976
New York magazine
AD: Milton Glaser

1 My painting of the exterior of the disco in Bay Ridge, Brooklyn, where I photographed the research for my paintings.

2, 3 Two of more than 500 photographs I took in the discos of Bay Ridge.

4, 5 My first small experimental painting and the research photograph.

6 A pencil sketch in which I considered combining the information from three different photos, an approach I abandoned.

In the winter of 1975, Milton Glaser called me up to say he had a project for *New York* magazine that he thought might interest me: to accompany writer Nik Cohn to a number of discotheques in Brooklyn, gathering visual reference material for pictures while Cohn gathered information for an article. It sounded intriguing, and so Cohn and I met to discuss it further. Nik had the idea that young people who were going to discos outside Manhattan were listening to an entirely different kind of music than that being promoted by major record companies such as Columbia. He wanted to do a story on what he believed was a new phenomenon flourishing unnoticed fifteen minutes away from Manhattan: a major resurgence of 1950s greaser style, both in clothes and in behavior. I didn't know enough about the current music business to have any particular insight into his theory, but the safari attracted me and we agreed to start looking around the clubs of Brooklyn the next weekend.

When Nik and I met the following week, he was accompanied by a black disco dancer named "Toute Suite," whom he had written about previously in *New York* magazine in relation to a dance contest. Toute Suite was tall, skinny, good-looking, and talkative, and he gave the impression of having smiled his way into and out of a great many adventures. He was to be our guide into the netherworld of Brooklyn discos, Nik explained.

With Toute Suite giving directions, I drove the three of us to the Bay Ridge section Brooklyn. We went first to the 2001 Club, which was a cavernous, cheaply decorated place with a large, shiny black dance floor and tiers of tables rising up at the back of the room. The place had once been a supper club, and we could see the vestiges of its other life in the Mediterranean-style wrought iron that fenced each level. Panels of Mylar hung from the walls, and Christmas lights blinked here and there. It did not evoke the futuristic perfection the club's name led me to expect, but it was an interesting space to walk around in. The place was not crowded when we arrived, and since Toute Suite was anxious to show us several more places which he assured us were better, we moved on.

Ironically, "better" apparently meant whiter, for the next two clubs we visited had almost none of the Hispanic or Black faces we had seen among others at 2001. Both of these clubs were more slickly decorated than 2001, with fairly complex lighting and overwhelming sound systems. I was still moving through the crowds with very little idea of what I might make of the experience. The incredibly loud music and the disorienting flash of the lights numbed my mind, and I followed in the wake of Toute Suite and Nik, hoping it would all become clear to me later.

By the time we reached the third club, we had all had a few drinks and Toute Suite was in a very manic mood. I was off on my own in this club, looking over the crowd and surreptitiously taking a photograph or two, and so I only noticed Toute Suite occasionally. At some point Nik was at my elbow pointing out Toute Suite on the dance floor doing his champion stuff with a young Italian girl. Nik said, "Watch that guy over there. He's looking at Toute Suite as though he could kill him." Sure enough, a stocky red-haired guy was staring malevolently at Toute Suite, and as I watched he jumped forward and slugged Toute Suite across the side of the head. Suddenly, a pack of male bodies disengaged from the larger mass and surrounded Toute Suite. They all wanted to get into the fight so much that they were jumping all over each other, and this got them so off balance that the whole group fell to the floor. It happened very

1

2

3

4

5

6

quickly but, perhaps because of the effect of the strobe lights, the action seemed slow. Just as the tangle of bodies and jackhammer elbows reached the floor, three bouncers sliced through the confusion and deftly separated Toute Suite from his attackers. It was a triumph of technique over brute force. Nik and I tried to move toward the door through which Toute Suite had been escorted, but we couldn't shove our way between the bodies in front of us. Just then, a voice hissed at us to follow him to a rear fire door. When this representative of the management got us to the sidewalk, he told us to get Toute Suite the hell out of there. Nik went to collect Toute Suite, and I ran three blocks to get the car. As I careened up to the entrance of the disco, a bouncer and Nik were trying to restrain Toute Suite, who was threatening to go back in and take on the whole club. Nik finally got him into the car and I gunned her away. Toute Suite had a cut lip but was otherwise okay. In the car, he talked of coming back the next night with his people, but I knew this was the end of the incident. We drove back into Manhattan, and I joined Nik and Toute Suite for a drink at a Black disco.

Two things that happened as a result of that evening were important. One was that all my film came back totally dark from the processor, and I faced the fact that I couldn't shoot my pictures with available light. I decided to use a flash for subsequent shooting. The second was that I realized Nik knew little more about the clubs than I did, and his dependence on Toute Suite as a guide showed me that I would now have to follow my own instincts in researching the disco scene. From the experience so far I could see that what either of us would get from the clubs was going to be very different from Nik's first thesis.

Although I now knew I must use a flash to penetrate the darkness inside the clubs, it was not an easy switch to make. Because I want to maintain an impression of human observation in my work, I resist using a camera in any way that is dramatically different from the way I see the world without the camera. Although I do take advantage of the stop-action possibilities of a fast lens, I have for the most part limited myself to 35mm and 50mm lenses, which most closely approximate normal human vision. Besides having a prejudice against the extreme focal-length lenses, up to this point I had also resisted using a flash because of the flat, unreal quality it gives to photographs. Now that I was forced to buy a flash and use it for this assignment, I became curious about the possibilities it might open up.

Using a flash, even the rather amateur electronic kind I bought, also meant a different approach to being in the clubs. I could no longer drift around the fringes of the action, sneaking a shot when the occasion permitted. The flash would announce me vividly, and I would now have to match my style to this flamboyant equipment. When I went back alone the next weekend to two of the clubs we had visited, I decided on a frontal attack. In each case, I went up to the manager, identified myself as an artist researching for an article on Brooklyn discos for *New York* magazine, and asked permission to take photos of the club and its patrons. In both cases they said yes. Having gotten approval, I put myself in the role of the unstoppable professional. I apparently looked officially sanctioned, for as I moved around the clubs snapping pictures with great bursts of light, no one challenged me. Occasionally someone asked what I was doing, but very politely. It was as if the very assault of the flash had cowed even those who might have protested had I been taking ordinary available-light shots.

7

8

Brooklyn Disco

I had already decided that the 2001 Club interested me the most. Its diversity, even its tackiness, promised more human drama than the relative stiffness of the "better" clubs. Also, because the 2001 was big and made up of several different rooms, it was easier to move around in, and, because it had a bar separated from the noise of the main dance room, there was a place to which I could retreat for a quiet drink. I actually began to have a good time there—and though I never unbent enough to dance (I was too paranoid to leave the Nikon at a table), I did get myself into four-sentence conversations with various people. These small interactions and the hours spent watching the scene began to focus my reactions to life in the club. Shortly after the experience, I made some notes that describe my feelings this way:

At the very end of that first evening, I felt some other quality seep through the glistening crust of music, dance, and costume. By the second night at the clubs, I was aware that all this 'cool' was a mask concealing more familiar kinds of human connections: people didn't appear to be choosing partners for dancing and yet there was a sense of pairing off; everyone was even-tempered, almost disinterested, yet an undercurrent of hostility ran through the crowd; there was little obvious social exclusion in the fluid intermingling of the people in the club, but there were flashes of loneliness and isolation.

My notes also tell me that I shot seven rolls of Tri-X that first night I used the flash. Because of my blank film the first time around and my inexperience with the flash, I was nervous about how the shots would turn out. When I saw them, I was elated. Not only were most of them exposed correctly, but also the clarity and detail were very good. And when I really studied my contact sheets, I could see that certain nuances of gesture and expression which people had not bothered to hide in the dim light of the club had been caught in the flash and revealed in the photographs. The pictures unmasked subtle but definite shadings around people's eyes and mouths, as well as movements of their bodies, which supported the psychological undercurrents I had only intuited were there. In the photos, some people looked angrier or lonelier or more lost than I had remembered, but they expressed the sane moods I had guessed at. I also began to like the flatness of the photographs. Everyone within the range of the flash had been given the precision and weightlessness of a figure in a Japanese print. The weird hanging shadow that is unique to flash photos traced a demarcation along certain edges of the subject that was like an earthquake's crevice. The pictures looked false, but what they evoked was real.

When I spread the photographs out on my drawing table to look at them and make my sketches, my first reactions came out of many years of using photographs as reference: I started to shift information around and to combine details from several photos into one composition. Then I asked myself, why was I moving things around? These were *my* photographs and already part of my creative act—I could do anything I wanted with them, including using them pretty much as they were. This was quite a big change in my attitude toward the information, and it laid the basis for developing the way I painted the pictures.

In my first two sketches, I tried an energetic approach to the drawing and allowed the irregular shape of the painting to follow the rhythm of the subject matter. I wasn't satisfied with these sketches because they didn't seem to take advantage of the flat, Japanese printlike appearance of the photographs. I needed to

10

11

12

13

14

15

frame the information in order to exploit the patterning caused by the flash. My first sketch of the dancers was framed within a rectangle, but its large, close-up scale looked clumsy to me. However, my vision of what the paintings could be was beginning to come into focus—I saw them as precise, complex, silvery, rather flat images, almost like elegant puzzles. I began painting from the group dancers photograph, changing the composition slightly so that the figures seem to dangle from the top edge of the painting, and I put more emphasis on the reflections on the floor. I had never painted so carefully or so slowly, but I was fairly sure I was onto something. It was very exhilarating. The painting took almost two weeks, and when I was through, I saw that my approach had worked.

Despite the fact that these paintings give a first impression that they are "photographically" accurate, the effort of having drawn them freehand is very important. Something expressive comes from all the minute changes, distortions, and simplifications that I make as I attempt to create the illusion of three-dimensional subject matter. All these small variations are part of my effort to understand and assimilate the photograph's information. When I draw a line describing part of the surface of an arm, for instance, I am not simply copying the boundary of an area from the photograph, I am also synthesizing what I understand about *arm*, which envelops a larger experience than my observation of that particular arm. Drawing, whether I use it naturalistically or in some stylized way, is a large part of my creative opportunity. I do not use any means of photographic projection to cut short the drawing process because it would eliminate much of the drawing's expressiveness.

I am convinced that this process can result in a painting that expresses a great deal more than the photograph it resembles. A photo is a true fragment of a complete action captured by the camera. I think it is possible for a painting based on a photograph to become an image with a larger meaning, so that rather than being a fragment cut from the whole, it appears to stand for the whole. This enrichment in the painting happens because as the artist understands and assimilates the photographic reality, his or her thoughts and attitudes about the whole scene flow imperceptibly into each esthetic choice. I believe that my disco paintings are emotionally energized by the amount of time I spent making and thinking about them.

The disco assignment gave me the most freedom and responsibility I had ever had in deciding what I would make of my subject, and it led me to invent a new kind of painting to express the sense of alienation and hostility that I felt existed in the disco clubs. The experience was a turning point for me in some way that I do not altogether understand, but I think it has something to do with liberating feelings in my work that had never seemed appropriate when I was illustrating someone else's text.

When I had completed the first painting, Milton Glaser met with me and was enthusiastic about what I was doing. I didn't see Nik Cohn after our club visits in January until I took the finished paintings to *New York* magazine one day in March. We spoke briefly, and he told me he was having writer's block about the story. For the next two months, it was not clear whether he would ever finish it, but finally, and fortunately, he did. When my pictures and Nik's story ran in the June 7, 1976, issue of *New York* magazine, they attracted the attention of producer Robert Stigwood, who used their aura and imagery as the basis for the movie *Saturday Night Fever.*

16

Teamsters

November 7, 1976
The New York Times Magazine
AD: Ruth Ansel

My growing impulse to simplify the concepts of my illustration and to express the ideas of the text with carefully staged but straightforward realism runs counter to two strong expectations about illustration: that it will show magical connections between things and that it will not overlap the territory of photography. Many editors and some art directors have difficulty understanding why I would want to paint a figure based on a photograph without doing something to the image that is beyond the technical range of the camera. I feel, of course, that I do just that—I add emotional and esthetic qualities that don't exist in the original photograph. The skeptics aren't talking about those kinds of things, however—they mean, why don't I bend the figure's arm in some impossible way, or add a mysterious landscape that appears to inhabit the figure's chest cavity, or some such sleight of hand? By choosing to omit surrealistic elements in most of my recent work, I have created a question in the minds of some people I deal with—what is my illustration doing that a photograph couldn't do? It is a hard position to defend because if a client does not feel the emotional power that comes out of this handling of realism, there is not much other information I can add to justify the approach.

A question like this arose in the early stages of my doing a cover on the teamster's union for the Sunday *New York Times Magazine.* The art director, Ruth Ansel, wanted me to do a painting in the style of the disco series, which she understood involved a particular way of seeing the subject. We had discussed the fact that it was important for me, in doing this kind of picture, that the subject be caught in the middle of unremarkable actions that implied rather than explained particular states of mind. It was just this aspect of my approach which raised a question in the mind of the editor. When I explained my idea of illustrating the dangerously growing power of the union by doing a portrait of a trucker in a truck, the editor was dubious. How could such a simple image say so much? He had imagined, he told us, an illustration on the cover in which a formation of trucks comes flying over the horizon like B-29s about to bomb the countryside. What he was imagining, of course, was illustration doing its classic job—showing something that is magical and can't be photographed. I agreed that, although this could be a good cover, it was not a concept that I was interested in doing. With Ruth's help, I finally persuaded the editor to let me proceed with the sketch that I had described. He insisted that my picture should at least show the truck driver talking to a union official to give it a greater sense of story. Against my own instinct, I agreed to include a second figure in the sketch.

For the sketch, which was due the next day, I didn't have time to take photographs. In the interim, I used a picture from a book on truckers as my research. The shot had a good, ominous, nighttime feeling about it and a hint of aggression in the driver's face which was just right. I added a business-suited figure at the bottom of the composition which, for me, created more questions about the picture than it answered.

After seeing the sketch, the editor was somewhat more convinced of the possibilities of this approach. Fortunately, he agreed that the figure of the union official didn't add to the meaning of the picture, but he still felt that the trucker alone was not enough. Ruth saved the day by thinking of adding the teamsters' logo as a second element, which I thought was a good idea and so did the editor.

I could now arrange to take my own photographs. My first task, finding a model, turned out to be easy because a carpenter who worked in the loft below my studio was as good a type for this role as I was likely to find, and he was enthusiastic about posing. I remember that he showed me three jackets that he could wear for my photographs. None of them was quite right, but I settled on a shiny red jacket, thinking to myself that I could change the color later and subdue some of its plastic cheeriness. I thought then that red was too bright and possibly too decorative a color for a tough trucker.

We used the trucks in the *New York Times* loading area. They were not the monumental, rivet-sided transcontinental sixteen-wheelers I had imagined, but in the one evening I had in which to take the photos, they were good enough. The poses we tried were all variations of my model sitting in or getting out of the truck. I finally decided to use one of the latter poses because I liked the idea of the man advancing on the viewer and his head breaking the line of the truck roof. Because the door was open, I had to give up showing the complicated struts and supports of the rear-view mirror which were a big "truck" clue in the photographs; so, in my painting, I moved the chromium climbing handle closer to the door and into the picture to strengthen the identity of the truck.

As I began painting the picture, I realized that the red jacket could be a strong, evocative element. It suggested, both in its primary color and in the agitated shapes of its wrinkles, a sense of uneasy hostility. There was a point in the painting where the jacket was paler, pink really, and very beautiful. I pressed on with my layers of paint, however, knowing somehow that I wouldn't get away with a pink-jacketed trucker. The whole painting is more layered and worked than the disco pictures. I felt it needed this density and darkness to work as a magazine cover and to stand up to the inevitable softening of the image that would occur when it was printed on newsprint.

Although as I paint I'm not really conscious of how the colors and values I use will pick up in the separations or print in a magazine, I have a general idea of how dark or bright something should be in order to survive the reproduction process. Much of my work is on the pale end of the spectrum as far as illustration goes, however, and for years I have resisted the pressure in one way or another to radically brighten or accentuate my art. Watercolor has a natural range of color and tonality based on its transparency and the fact that it gets its luminescence from the light going through the medium and bouncing off the white paper underneath. When you try to deepen the color beyond a certain point, it becomes almost opaque and loses its brilliance. Years ago I tried using dyes because of their much brighter color, but I found that, besides not liking the chemical kind of color, I couldn't really paint with dyes. Unlike watercolor, which tends to float on the surface of the paper, dyes sink right in, giving me no time to move and merge the medium. I think at that point, I realized that the paleness is as much a part of me as it is of the watercolor medium, and I would have to learn to use the quality so that it would become attractive to my audience.

Color is certainly important to this *New York Times* assignment, for as I consider the finished piece, I can see that it is my obvious involvement with describing the red jacket's labyrinthine folds and highlights that gives the cover its particular vitality. It is ironic but not unusual that an element such as this red jacket, which I first saw as a problem, should become the high point of the painting.

1 | I used this photo, from a book called *Trucker*, for my sketch.
2 | This sketch, which I showed to the art director and editor, included the requested "union official" figure.
3, 4 | Two of my research photos taken with a model and a *New York Times* delivery truck.

1

3

2

4

Teamsters

5

6

7

8

Pool Hustler

August 8, 1977
Sports Illustrated
AD: Richard Gangel

1   One of my photographs which I liked because of its long, stretched-out composition.
2   Pencil sketch using photo 1.
3   The photo that became the basic reference for my final painting.
4   A first pencil tryout of the image in photo 3.
5   An abandoned painting based on photo 1 with an additional figure.
6, 7   A photo of a cue-chalking player and a sketch including him.

Danny D. was a pool hustler. He traveled around the country making a very uneven living playing pool for money, sometimes with rubes and braggarts, but most often with other hustlers. It was a life of sleeping in cars and spending a lot of time in lurid poolrooms at the edges of cities.

I was assigned to illustrate Danny D.'s story for *Sports Illustrated*. Despite the fact that the article was based on a real character, I decided that trying to actually reconstruct the scenes described in the manuscript would lead to stiff, unconvincing images. The art director, Richard Gangel, agreed with me that my illustration would be more exciting if I watched real-life games and then made my paintings from my observations. We both felt I could capture the fundamental drama of pool-playing with the eyewitness method: even though Danny D. moved from town to town, finding new challenges and new terms for each game, the moment the men circled the pool table and each other, the duel became a classic and unchanging confrontation.

Pool hustlers are worlds away from those smiling smoothies you see in ads for home pool tables, and they are even farther away from the vested old boys chalking up in the manor house. Pool hustling teeters on that ramshackle fence between the criminal and straight worlds—the territory, in fact, where all con games operate. The pool hall is a cliché come true, the den of iniquity that, from Victorian times, young men have been warned to avoid.

The assignment was beautiful in its simplicity, I thought. If I could just take some great photos in the real pool halls of the city, I would have the research for a tough, true painting. There was, however, an aspect to this assignment that gave me trepidation. I pictured myself walking into some establishment on Eighth Avenue in New York City with my camera ready, facing a room full of pool hustlers with God knows how many reasons for not wanting to have their pictures taken. I somehow knew that whatever wicked reputation the Victorian imagination had ascribed to pool halls, and whatever infamy they may have earned in other cities, the pool halls of Manhattan would be much, much worse. This assignment, I realized, was my most dangerous so far in terms of photographing out in the world, and the apprehension I felt about throwing myself into this alien group touched off an old childhood fear.

I was born in China before World War II and spent the war years moving between China, Canada, and India. All that traveling meant changing schools frequently, and in each of these situations, I experienced the terrors of being the new boy. There is a classic and heroic way of entering a new group and winning its respect and approval—by fighting one of its leaders. This was never one of my options, however, since I was neither assured enough physically to win the fight nor masochistic enough to accept the inevitable defeat. Gradually I developed my own way to win a place in each group, or to at least avoid most of the bullying that often awaits the newcomer: I traded on my exoticism.

I found if I could dramatize the accent of the country I had just come from and appear to be filled with its arcane knowledge, I could intimidate the other boys into looking upon me with puzzled awe and, if I were lucky, respect. The technique depended on my being essentially quiet and "deep," and occasionally on telling farfetched stories that would add spice to my somewhat austere performance. In this way I survived to adulthood.

Now, many years and lands later, I found myself on the brink of entering another potentially dangerous group. This time it

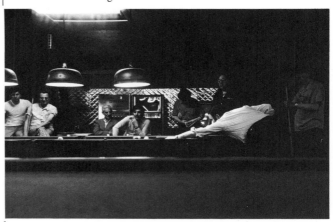

1

2

3

4

5

6

7

was the gang in the pool parlor. I wondered whether my technique of dramatized strangeness would work in a world that knew a little more about strangeness than my knee-socked cohorts in Darjeeling.

Certainly the role I would have to play now was a more assertive one—I needed to approach and mingle with these men. I also needed to photograph them, which could prove to be a problem. To minimize the camera's presence, I bought myself a Leica CL, which was not only much quieter than my old Nikon but also had a black case that was smaller and looked less professional. Outfitted with my new camera and dressed in conservative clothes, I was ready to hit the beachhead on Eighth Avenue. I hoped I looked like an intense intellectual on a photo mission of not much worldly importance.

I arrived at the pool hall and descended the stairs to a cavernous room below street level. There were about thirty-five men standing around or playing pool in a room that could hold about a hundred. I went immediately to the manager, who was sitting in a partitioned office near the entry, and told him I was an illustrator researching a story on pool halls for a magazine. I was somewhat vague on the assignment and the magazine, but he didn't seem to care. All he understood was that it might mean some publicity, and he said, "Sure, take what you want," adding that he couldn't speak for the patrons.

I walked slowly around the room now, giving everyone a chance to check me out and to see the camera around my neck. I didn't take any pictures on this circuit and, in fact, I wandered for quite some time before I attempted a photograph. The kinds of players in the place ranged from hard-bitten old men to easygoing Greeks to flashily dressed young dudes who looked, as the saying goes, as if they kept their own counsel.

Whenever I found a group I wanted to photograph, I would stand quietly watching them for some time. I would then approach the most outgoing, flamboyant player and ask if he minded my taking a few shots of him. In every case but one the answer was "No, I don't mind." I would start shooting from close in (using Tri-X film and available light), obviously concentrating on this person, but when I felt everyone was used to me and my camera, I would back up to include more and more figures.

I spent about three hours in the pool hall that night, sometimes sitting and watching for as long as fifteen minutes without taking a shot. I didn't try to talk to or jolly up the customers. Occasionally someone would ask what I was doing with the photos, but because one of his pool-playing buddies would always answer for me—"You're going to be the centerfold for *Playgirl*!"—I never really had to deal with the question seriously.

The experience had been surprisingly easy. Perhaps it was dumb luck, or perhaps I had romantically anticipated a tougher breed than I actually encountered. The photographs, however, had just the ominous grittiness I had hoped for; it was a little difficult to believe I had moved through the company of these hard-faced men with such aplomb.

Turning these photographic images into a painting involved some trial-and-error sketching to decide which of two shots I would use as my basic reference. At first I was attracted to the long horizontal composition of photo 1, which presented the players in a dark tableau that reminded me of Da Vinci's *Last Supper.* As you can see from sketch 5, I added a foreground figure and a player on the left-hand end of the table (both of them taken from other photographs) to give the picture more depth and a sense of complete action. When I looked at what I had done, however, I wasn't satisfied. Perhaps the foreground figure was a mistake, as it diluted the horizontal effect that had attracted me to the photo in the first place. In any case, as I considered this sketch, it seemed to lack a central action that could hold the complicated scene together. One sees several men watching a game, but the game itself is hardly visible in the picture.

The appeal of photo 3 for me was the clear image of the man playing the ball on the table surface and the complete view of his pose. It took me two sketches to realize that I could simplify the foreground space into a diagrammatic drawing of the floor tiles. Doing this helped me focus the picture on the player and dramatized the diagonal movement into space. The solidity of the scene establishes itself increasingly as one moves up the page, suggesting an entrance to the scene—linear and fragmentary as you step onto the first few tiles, a combination of lines and color as you move past the player and the table, and an almost impenetrable tone as you reach the onlookers in the back of the room. It is an illustration about mood and a certain kind of tough guy, and pictorially, it relies on a simple spatial illusion for its drama.

When I finished this pool hustler painting, I felt a certain kind of satisfaction that I enjoy from time to time—that my lengthy refinement of a basically simple realistic scene has resulted in an emotionally charged and esthetically interesting illustration. In other words, all my fussing with a series of subtle changes has been worth it. Sometimes, however, these works for which I feel such affection seem to leave my audience unimpressed. Occasionally, even I grow to feel that my esthetic games in these pictures may have been too private to matter. This is a disturbing insight to have, since the finely tuned realistic picture is probably my most natural form of expression, but it is also the form in which I walk the narrowest line between unique success—a realism that evokes complex psychological moods—and banal failure—or realism that evokes the subject and nothing more. When I am deeply involved in one of these pictures, I feel exhilarated not only by being in touch with a vision that has strong evocative possibilities but also by going against the grain of most contemporary artistic enthusiasms—decorative patterning, stylization of forms, and simplification. But when I fail to make the picture sufficiently evocative, my work seems connected to the dispirited, sentimental realism I dislike. Sometimes, when I have just finished a piece of art, it is not immediately clear to me on which side of the fence the piece has fallen. But in the case of the pool hustler painting, I had a very strong feeling that I had succeeded, and as time passed, I was gratified to see that many people agreed with me. I make this point about my audience's acceptance of the pool hustler painting—as measured by the unscientific but generally accurate yardstick of response from friends and the work's inclusion in various juried exhibitions—because the piece is so special. After all, I am trying to convince the world that an illustration which is very much like a lot of pedestrian pictures is essentially different and more charged with meaning than these other paintings. I am asking the audience to respond to an ineffable quality that lies beyond merely illustrating the action and the vitality of a scene—a quality that I struggle to express through a long-winded process of sketches and reconsiderations. When one of these paintings of simple but personal realism, such as the pool hustler illustration, succeeds, it pleases me more than the success of a theatrical poster or record album which after all, has a more accessible kind of drama.

8 | The color sketch that resolved color and value in this composition.

9 | A refinement of sketch 8, pulling out the right-hand figure slightly.

10 | (*Overleaf*) The painting as it ran in *Sports Illustrated*.

8

9

10

Aging Hustler

December 3, 1979
New York magazine
AD: J. C. Suarès

This illustration for a story by Orde Coombs of an aging male hustler is probably the most effective cover I ever did for *New York* magazine in terms of its drama and newsstand appeal, but ironically, I have reservations about it as a painting. In making the color and tonal values emphatic enough to satisfy the generally accepted idea of cover "punch," I overpainted the picture. Given the kind of editorial nervousness and scrutiny surrounding magazine covers, it was not surprising that I fell into this trap.

Because so much of a magazine's economic survival depends on newsstand sales, editorial meetings on covers are usually enlivened by a great deal of conjecture about what makes a good one. Sometimes this opinion is bolstered by the pseudo-science of sales figures or reader surveys ("The color purple anywhere on the cover will doom it"), but more often it is the anxious and unadorned intuition of the editor ("I don't like that nose").

In my own experience, the paleness of my painting and the subtlety of my ideas are the two factors that have been called into question the most. I have probably done a cover or two that were too pale, but I can't really agree with the second criticism. Whenever I have modified my idea to make it more "obvious" the cover has usually been second-rate; in those cases where I stuck to my guns or where my "subtle" idea was accepted (as in the cover on the teamsters' union), the final art was dramatic and coherent. In the present instance, I had control over both the concept and the painting, but some anxiety garnered over the years in battles about paleness led me to overemphasize the edges of this painting and complicate the forms of the face and arms with too many layers of wash.

Nevertheless, I liked the story and took some trouble to find the right model. The author had described the main character, and so I knew what I was looking for—a thirty-six-year-old, 5′ 10″ Italian who was starting to lose his good looks and his confidence that he could continue to make a living from his wits and the selling of sexual favors. I hoped that Coombs's fictional story masked a real character, and so I phoned him to ask if he could help me find an appropriate model. He thought about my request for a while and then phoned me back with the name of a professional model. I arranged for this man to come see me and was astounded when he arrived: instead of the ruffian I expected, a smoothly handsome fellow walked in who was all wrong for the part. I then decided to try looking in the most obvious locale for my model, an infamous bar on New York's West Side where hustlers and their clientele get together. The bar was dimly lit, but not so dark that it prevented me from realizing that Coombs had given his hustler hero a totally unrealistic age. The young men here all appeared to be in their twenties, and those in their late twenties looked so burned out, either from drugs or from the rigors of their life, that it was hard to imagine any of them sustaining even the illusion of physical attractiveness into their middle thirties. I knew I would have to get my model in some other way.

As so often happens, the problem was solved almost accidentally and came to a quick conclusion. I happened to mention my search to an artist friend, and she said she had an ex-boyfriend who was perfect for the role. I met him that same evening. He agreed to model, and after picking up a tank top and a pair of jeans at his apartment, we took a cab to Times Square. There, amid the jibes of the real hustlers, male and female, I took many photos of my model, who fortunately turned out to be a good actor and a good sport.

1

2   3

4   5

Anna Christie

1977 Broadway play
Producer: Alexander H. Cohen

1   This photo of Greta Garbo as Anna Christie, from the 1930 movie, was my first piece of research.

2   A drawing I made from the photo simply to "try on" the image.

3–6   I sketched these ideas before taking any research photos.

7–10   Photos taken on a New York pier.

11   Sketch trying out the idea of the glistening black slicker.

12   Silhouette idea developed from photo 10.

In designing *Comedians*, my first poster for Broadway producer Alexander Cohen, I had to evoke a strange and ironic idea about comedy. My second Cohen poster, *Anna Christie*, presented me with the problem of dealing with a theatrical "chestnut."

Whatever else this Eugene O'Neill drama is, it is a classic of the American stage. Although the play's actual plot is only dimly remembered by most people, including myself, it is surrounded nevertheless by disconnected associations: "fallen woman," "tugboats," "drunken father," and lots of fog. I confess my own associations often led me to confuse *Anna Christie* with "Tugboat Annie," the series of stories that appeared in the *Saturday Evening Post* during the 1940s. (Forgive me, Eugene.)

Given the encrustation of history covering this play, it did not seem possible or even desirable to create a poster that did not acknowledge the aura the play already possessed in the minds of most people who would see it. Although I did not want to repeat anything that had been done in a previous *Anna Christie* poster, I did want to fulfill some of my audience's expectations—but in a very unexpected way.

Early in my research for the poster I came across an image in a photograph that kept coming back to me and finally affected my choices in the last stages of design. The photo was of Greta Garbo as Anna Christie, in the 1930 movie of the same name. Sitting at a table with her head heavily leaning on her hand, her sad eyes beautifully unfocused on the middle distance, she ignores the drink in front of her. It was a marvelous Garbo photograph and the only record I found of an *Anna Christie* production, either on stage or on screen, in which the heroine seemed psychologically modern enough for the dilemma in which O'Neill had placed her. Although much about the play is heavy and almost archaic, the story of the central character is decidedly modern. Garbo vividly expressed this spirit in the photograph and, as I look back on the path my choices took, I see that I tried to create my own version of what was so telling in Garbo's haunting slump.

If ever a contemporary actress was capable of reaching Garbo's level of psychological nuance (perhaps even surpassing it), it was the star of Cohen's *Anna Christie* production, Liv Ullmann. I was fortunate in having this great actress as the obvious focus of my poster, and from the first sketches I carefully considered the way she looked and moved. I studied dozens of photographs of her. In many of them she projected a spiritual pathos that I began to see as the central drama around which I could form my idea.

It would have been ideal at this stage to spend a day photographing Ullmann as she worked out the role. Something extraordinary would certainly have come of this; I could almost imagine some gesture, candid and unpredictable, which in its precise turn of body and expression would have given me the raw material for a unique image. The vitality of the human body, closely observed in its idiosyncracies, is what has always fascinated me about the posters of Toulouse Lautrec; it is this very lack of observation, the predictable simplification, that I find so boring in much of the poster art of our own time.

At this stage I started making pencil sketches based on my initial research from the library. I knew that I would eventually take my own photos, but I wanted to prepare myself for that step by immersing myself in images of previous productions of the play and of life on the Boston waterfront in the early 1900s. Often, the first page of my sketches also includes lists of words rep-

1

2

3

4

5

6

7

8

9

10

11

12

resenting my associations with the subject. They range from the obvious to the obscure; in the case of *Anna Christie*, from "fog" to "slicker shine." In my first sketches I played with various large heads of Anna Christie floating over seascapes or seen through a porthole and the windows of a bar. I also sketched her seated sideways at a table and again standing desolately on a wharf, with her reflection broken up by the choppy waters of Boston harbor. These first visualizations were connected by a mood of melancholy, the background of the sea, and the integration of the lettering into the painting. All of these elements were instinctive and interesting to me, and in one way or another they survived to the final version of the poster.

The fact that melancholy was the appropriate mood for an image representing this play made my invention especially enjoyable. A melancholic quality seems to seep into my work from time to time whether or not I intend to put it there, and so it was liberating to be able to use a psychology that is apparently natural to me. The recurrence of the sea in most of my sketches is not surprising, given the locale and the symbolism of the play itself, but it also reflects my own obsession with water. I have managed to include water subjects in a great variety of assignments ranging from my Big Apple poster to the final project in this book, the water pistol on the *Graphis* cover. If this preoccupation signifies some aberration in my early toilet training, I am, thankfully, not aware of it. I think it is much more likely that I am fascinated by water, since manipulating it is so much a part of my medium. My decision to letter the title as part of the painting reflects my general opinion that my work looks better with my own lettering than it does with headline type.

As I had suspected from the first, I wanted the kind of image that comes only from watching and photographing a model as she acts and moves. Since Ullmann was in Europe and unavailable, I arranged to take the photos with a stand-in. Certainly, I could find the pose that would give me my central image and later photograph Ullmann in the same pose to give me the particular information for the portrait. (Obviously, I reread the play in search of those scenes that might best convey a powerful image of it as a poster.) I am fortunate to have a beautiful friend, Elena Pavlov, who resembles Liv Ullmann in a general way. Elena agreed to pose, and, with a suitcase full of clothes we believed to be "of the period," we set out to photograph at two locations.

The first was an abandoned wharf on Manhattan's Lower West Side. We got there about one chilly hour before sunset, as that was the kind of light I had imagined in certain scenes of the play. Elena posed leaning against pilings, with and without a suitcase, sometimes wearing just a short jacket over her dress and sometimes enveloped in a seaman's large black slicker. I photographed innumerable variations of several poses and also asked a male friend to pose with Elena for a series of shots. The light was fading all this time, and so the last shots were virtual silhouettes. Since it was harder to invent plausible "actions" on this barren wharf than I had imagined, the suitcase became an important actor—it was the only prop with which Elena could really interact.

When the light faded entirely, we moved on to our second location: an old bar in Little Italy with the kind of woodwork and other details that placed it in the right era without appearing so precious as to be unbelievable as a working-man's bar on the Boston waterfront. It was nearly empty when we arrived, and the

owner had no objections to our monopolizing his back room for a photo session. The bar was an easier situation in which to work. It was warm, for one thing, while it had been very cold outside. We drank beer as we took the pictures, and I felt good about Elena's acting as she moved around the room and sat at the table. All in all, I took seven rolls of film that day.

When the contact prints from this shooting were ready, I chose to have about a dozen photos, picked equally from the shots taken at both locations, to be printed in the 8″ x 10″ size (20.3 x 25.4 cm). With these twelve images, I worked for three days making small drawings in pencil. Making these sketches, in addition to providing an opportunity to compose within the rectangular shape of the poster, gave me time to absorb the information in the photographs. Sometimes when I make drawings from photographs I don't try to *design* at all, but simply search out the visual structure of the information. In this particular instance, at the end of three days I had narrowed my choices down to two interior poses and was now ready to do some color sketches.

Why did I reject the oudoor scenes? Well, for two practical reasons and because my hopes for one of the outdoor ideas had not panned out. The practical reasons were that the good shots of Elena with the other model were all horizontal images that did not adapt well to the vertical format of the poster. Also, I felt in many of the outdoor shots Elena was merely posing. My inability to find a rationale for her movements in that "barren landscape" had produced photos in which Elena's figure did not look "motivated," to use actors' parlance.

The idea that didn't pan out had to do with the seaman's black slicker. I had envisioned Anna Christie's pale, lovely head emerging from the darkness of her oversize coat, which I had imagined with a wonderful complication of glistening wrinkles. I had anticipated a dramatic juxtaposition of the smooth-skinned face with a voluminous, anthracite form. To make all of it come true, I had gone to an army–navy surplus store and bought the most convincing working-man's black slicker I could find. The color was right, but the fabric was very, very smooth— apparently some new kind of vinyl that never shows a crease. No amount of rubbing, crinkling, or jumping on it could in any way trouble its placid surface. Instead of the zigzag jumble of highlights I had conjured for this coat, all I got were broad, uninteresting planes of brand-new-looking fabric. Elena did look as if she had borrowed her father's coat, but it was in no way sexy or mysterious.

I began working instead with the inside shots, which had a convincing quality to them. Elena was obviously more comfortable, her movements in the bar more logical, and the play of light more dramatic and appropriate to the subject. I began by working on an image of Elena walking into the light of the bar, holding her suitcase. She seemed caught in that moment when all of Anna Christie's apprehension about entering this new situation is revealed. She holds the suitcase up to her body as though she must defend herself; the way her hand touches her hat suggests that she suddenly feels the hat is a pretension she can't carry off. The pool of light is like an arena into which she has just stepped with uncertainty. The image had all the qualities I wished to capture by photographing a person "acting." After working with this image awhile, I realized it had one serious problem. If I were really going to utilize its figure-in-space qualities, that is, if I were to include enough of the room for the viewer

13 | This sketch was my last attempt to use outdoor staging.
14 | One of several photos shot in a bar in Little Italy.
15 | An intermediate design based on photo 14.
16 | In this last sketch, based on photo 14, I invented the paint-stroke idea that I used in the final artwork.

13

14 15

16

Anna Christie

to really feel the character entering it, the face would be too small for an adequately dramatic portrait of Liv Ullmann. I finally decided to go on to the more intimate image of Anna sitting at the table.

Despite my decision to abandon the previous idea, I realized that in developing it I had already made a small but important graphic invention. It was in many ways the most enjoyable bit of creating I did for this poster. When drawing the pencil sketches, I made fast oblique strokes as a shorthand indication of where a dark tonal passage behind the figure would fade out. I meant to suggest a rather straightforward watercolor wash that went from dark to light, but then I became intrigued with the character of the strokes themselves. I experimented with them in paint and also began incorporating the lettering as a continuation of the movement and spirit of the strokes. The arbitrariness of the idea fascinated me. It allowed me to combine two scenes without rationalizing them spatially. I didn't have to provide, for instance, a fortuitous window behind or beside the figure to show both the interior of the bar and the all-important sea outside. With these fast, almost slapdash strokes, I could let the dark interior simply seem to paint itself over the seascape (like the Sherwin Williams logo, in which a can of paint tips out its contents onto a globe of the world). For me, this energetic calligraphy became the most unique characteristic of the design.

Having solved the treatment of the lettering and exterior-interior combination, I began working with the photographs of the seated Anna. Designing the image went fairly quickly—the figure and the table seemed to "call out" for a particular position and scale in the poster. Most of the refining I did on these sketches consisted of adjusting the color and form. I was satisfied at this point that I had a sketch I could show to the producer, Alex Cohen.

Cohen is not a man given to fiddling with things; he either feels they are essentially right, or they are wrong. He was delighted with the design. He wanted no changes at all and later, when the costume designer objected to the green color of the dress in my sketch as being "wrong for the period, wrong for O'Neill, and wrong for Miss Ullmann," Alex Cohen agreed with me that it was "right for the poster." He also agreed that it was important for me to take photographs of Ullmann in a hat and in the right light so my portrait of her would really be in the spirit of the sketch. He arranged a meeting with her and, fortunately, she liked the sketch. She looked at it intently for a few seconds and then turned her incredible face toward me and said, "You know me already."

The photographs I took of her were fairly simple head-and-shoulder portraits, and I tried to pose Miss Ullmann in such a way that she repeated the body line of my photographs of Elena Pavlov. Once I had the prints from this shooting, I made some small color studies and then proceeded to paint the final poster.

It was printed and displayed on hundreds of railroad stations in the commuter ring around New York—my *Anna Christie* poster showing Liv Ullmann staring out at the world from behind her bar table. In the winding path of my search for the right image for the poster, I had tried Anna bundled in a black slicker against the dusky waters of the Hudson River, posed her with her lover, and placed her standing in the gloom of a downtown bar; but eventually I had made the decision to pose her very much like the first piece of research I had looked at—the 1930 photograph of Greta Garbo.

17

18

19

20

21

Anna Christie

22–24 | Three of the photos that I took of Liv Ullmann in preparation for the portrait.
25 | A portrait study I did to warm up for the final painting.
26 | The printed poster.

22

23

24

25

Ain't Misbehavin'

1979 Broadway play
Ash/LeDonne Inc.
AD: Jeff Ash

In designing the poster for *Ain't Misbehavin'*, based on the life and music of Fats Waller, I had the distinct advantage of seeing the musical before I started to work. Very seldom, of course, does an artist doing theatrical posters actually see the work performed before his design is finished, since the poster is part of the advance publicity for the event; but in the case of *Ain't Misbehavin'*, I was designing for a show that was moving from Off Broadway to On. This meant that I could see the performance at the Manhattan Theater Club prior to its move to the Longacre Theater on 48th Street. Therefore, instead of trying to think up images culled from a script and publicity shots of the stars, I was able to remember the effect and the spirit of the actual singing and dancing I had seen. And what dancing I remembered! I loved the whole show, but I will never forget the shaking and shimmying of one cast member in particular. Her name is Nell Carter, and the way she moved her generous physique as she acted and danced out the ribald lyrics of Fats Waller was a totally unique blend of style, sass, sex, and sense of humor. In Nell's rare moments of stillness, her body appeared to be too short and thick to do the tremulous quivers and earthshaking grinds that it obviously did do, which made the effect of her dancing even more voluptuous and magical. It was a perfect evocation of the bawdy sophistication of Fats Waller's songs.

I was not able to photograph in the theater, and the official performance photographs did not capture Nell Carter's extraordinary, compacted energy. This was neither a surprise nor a great problem to me because Nell Carter had given me such a clear vision of what I wanted in my painting that I knew I would get it one way or another. Even my first pencil and wash sketches, invented without much help from reference photos, have a lot of spirit simply because of my memories of the performance. In fact, struggling to draw a dancing Fats Waller woman from my imagination gave me a chance to figure out what gave the body moves their zing. It had a lot to do with the accentuated hips and the wide stance of the legs. I remembered too, that Carter's dress had been tight and had cooperated with the choreography somewhat reluctantly. It had also been short, and when she danced, it hitched up high so that it formed a tight loop around her thighs.

I asked a dancer friend, Claire Brooks, to pose for some research photos. Although Claire has a slim-waisted body and is white, I was confident that she could move in a way that would recreate the spirit of the generously proportioned Black dancers of *Ain't Misbehavin'*. I was right. After changing into the dress I had rented from an antique clothing store, and with a little coaching from me, Claire began to move to the music with great oomph. All of the connections and emphasis I was looking for were in Claire's dancing and in the photos I took of her.

Although the producers of the show liked my sketch and thought it really captured the special flavor of the performance, they were concerned that my image didn't represent the show as a "big" musical. I added one more figure in the background and they approved the art, which was then used in a newspaper ad and as a two-color poster.

The producer's reservations about the poster's intimate tone finally won out, however, and they commissioned Doug Johnson to do another piece of art which successfully emphasized the style and implicit scale of *Ain't Misbehavin'*. I like Doug's poster and see that it is probably a better marketing tool than mine, but I still feel that my dancing figure successfully evokes a unique quality of Fats Waller's music.

1

2

3

4–8

9

10

11 | Studies of the head and hairdo.
12 | Art as it ran in the *New York Times*.
13 | Color sketch for the poster, which was never produced.

11

12

TV Shakespeare

1978
McCaffrey and McCall, Inc.
AD: Susan Lyster

1 | The ad-agency sketch prepared before I was given the assignment.
2 | A color doodle to help me exorcise the agency's juggler idea.
3 | An early version of Shakespeare raising the curtain on his plays.
4–6 | Some pencil sketches of Shakespeare writing, looking amazed, and doing magic tricks.
7 | A sketch influenced by photographs I once saw of Picasso drawing in the air with a flashlight.

One of the most potentially creative assignments an illustrator can get is a commission to design a poster advertising one of the shows sponsored by large corporations on public television. The work pays relatively well, usually offers a strong subject for illustration, and is widely published and exhibited.

This was the kind of assignment I was offered by the McCaffrey and McCall agency. Susan Lyster, the art director, called me to say they wanted me to do an introductory poster for a series of Shakespeare plays co-sponsored by Exxon and Morgan Guaranty Trust Company. When we met at her office, Susan showed me a color sketch she had designed. The black-bordered composition was of a magicianlike Shakespeare juggling a series of characters from his plays. Although it was ingenious enough as a poster idea, I recognized that it had been taken, with only slight changes, from a School of Visual Arts poster Milton Glaser had done several years before. I said I thought it was pointless for me to deal with such rich subject matter if I didn't have the creative space to come up with my own solution. Susan explained that the job had originally been designated for Milton, but because of a series of complications, he was not going to do it. However, the client had already seen and liked the agency comp. Because I felt so strongly about inventing my own metaphor for this poster, Susan and I discussed how much changing of their original concept she would accept. I finally convinced her that if I kept the basic dark framing of the design and a central figure of Shakespeare, the client could probably accept it.

With this understanding, I started to work. My first doodles were of other juggling figures, not because I had any intention of using this concept but as a way of exorcising the image from my mind. I went on to every other idea I could think of in which a figure of Shakespeare introduces his plays. The first sketch that satisfied me was of a song-and-dance Shakespeare with a huge quill under his arm and play characters streaming from his hat. The art director and the creative director both seemed delighted with the sketch. After a few days, however, they got back to me with the news that Exxon's advertising manager felt something was wrong with the sketch that was beyond verbalizing. When they asked me to think some more about the problem, I had the idea of showing Shakespeare holding back a curtain—perhaps the shadowed curtain itself could form the dark frame for the design and Shakespeare could stand almost silhouetted by the light of the stage behind him. I tried this, and it worked. When I showed them this sketch, both the agency and the client were pleased—with one "small" change: in order to strengthen the TV context, they wanted me to add a camera and cameraman behind the figure of Shakespeare. I protested that this would disastrously complicate the image, but they persisted so vigorously in their argument that I said I would bring them a sketch with the camera added so that they could see for themselves that it was a bad idea. I brought in the amended sketch, the client loved it, and the idea was approved.

I took a research photograph of the figure of Shakespeare pushing back the curtain, but before I even got my prints back, Susan Lyster phoned me to say that because there was a dispute between Exxon and Morgan Guaranty Trust over the control of the advertising, no artwork or artist that had been commissioned by Exxon alone (which was the case here) could be used.

After all this fine-tuning of the idea, the job was cancelled for a reason having nothing to do with the quality of the art. As far as I know, no introductory poster was ever done.

SHAKESPEARE'S GREATEST HITS

36 PLAYS IN 6 YEARS ON PBS

1

2

3

4

5

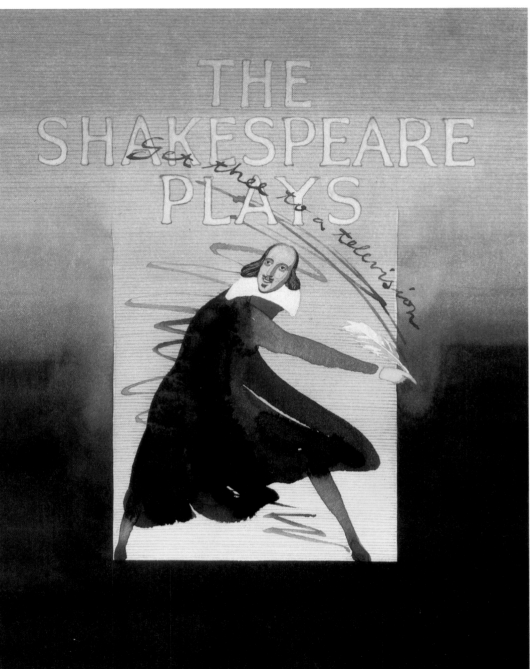

7

6

8

11

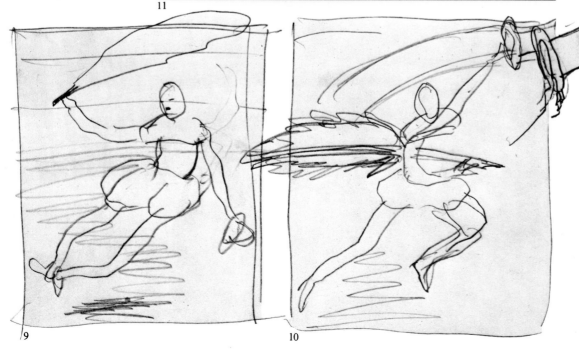

9

10

8–10 | Three pencil sketches inspired by pictures of Fred Astaire dancing.
11 | The color sketch that I developed from sketches 8–10 and which the client saw and rejected.
12 | Color study of Shakespeare in a cape.
13 | A model costumed as Shakespeare.
14 | First version of the Shakespeare and curtain idea.
15 | In this sketch I added the television camera that the client had requested.

14

12

13

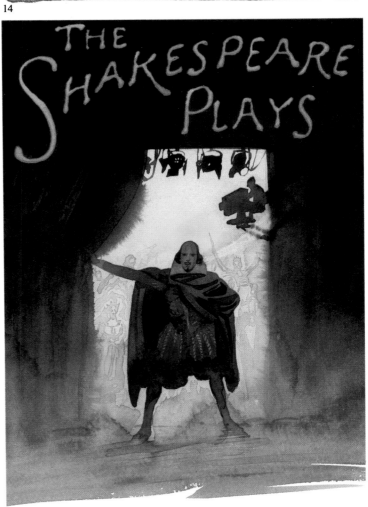

15

December 25, 1914

1978 animated film
Public Broadcasting System
Producer: R. O. Blechman

Like a lot of other artists, I have been both fascinated and repelled by animation. Fascinated, because it offers a method by which I can make my images connect and move to become part of this culture's most popular form of magic—film—and repelled, because in the commercial business of animation, the method Walt Disney developed in the 1920s is seen as the only viable way in which to get still art to move. Using this system, an artist must plan images so they can be painted on the slippery, impervious surface of a transparent sheet called a cel, and then the actual carrying out of the many individual pieces of art must be delegated to various artisan-specialists. Although artists constantly try to find new mediums that will adhere to the cel surface, nothing works as well as the black outline and flat opaque color Disney used for his cartoon films. At times I have tried to operate within these strictures. In designing three animated TV commercials, I reduced the complex texture of my work to flat areas of color and simplified my drawing so that it could be carried out by hands other than my own. Although some of the ideas for the animation were successful, it ultimately seemed pointless for me to be doing animation if I couldn't include the watercolor painting and the actual kind of drawing that makes my work unique. Despite these experiences, I have always felt that there is a way to conceive an animated film so that I could work on the paper surface I am comfortable with and reduce the number of drawings to an amount I could handle myself.

When Robert O. Blechman approached me in 1977 to design and execute a short film as part of a Christmas program he was producing for PBS-TV, I said I would be very interested in making a film if I could utilize my watercolor style of painting. He said that was exactly what he had in mind.

Bob's idea for the whole program was to choose literary and nonfiction pieces that were in one way or another about Christmas, but which addressed significant and sophisticated aspects of the subject. He wanted this TV hour to be in refreshing contrast to the saccharine programming that fills up most of the schedule at Christmastime. What he was planning was, in fact, an animated special for adults. The title he had chosen for the whole hour was *Simple Gifts*, and the other artists included were Seymour Chwast, Maurice Sendak, Charles Slackman, Philip Schopper, William Littlejohn, and Blechman himself.

The text he had chosen for me was a letter written by a young British captain, Sir Edward Hulse, to his mother, describing an extraordinary event in which he had participated on Christmas Day, 1914, on a trench battlefield in France. This actual event from World War I was a truce initiated by the foot soldiers of the opposing German and British armies that started on December 25 and ran for two days.

According to Captain Hulse's account of the truce, the firing from the German side died down early on Christmas morning, and at 8:30 A.M., four unarmed German soldiers approached the British trench. Captain Hulse went out to meet them, also unarmed. They told him that they had no feeling of enmity toward the English soldiers and had decided not to shoot again until the British did. The Captain and the Germans agreed to meet again in a larger group later in the afternoon, at which time, to quote Captain Hulse's letter:

> . . . this extraordinary scene was enacted between the lines: A German NCO with the iron cross, gained, he told me, for conspicuous skill in sniping, started his fellows off on some marching tune. When they had done I set the note for "The

Boys of Bonnie Scotland, Where the Heather and the Blue Bells Grow," and so we went on singing everything from "Good King Wenceslaus" down to ordinary Tommies' songs and ended up with "Auld Lang Syne," which we all, English, Scots, Irish, Prussian, Wurtemnbergs etc. joined in. It was absolutely astounding. . . .

Captin Hulse's letter about this fantastic event was simple and affecting, and as soon as I had read it I knew Bob Blechman had chosen well for me. My intuition told me that the spirit of this text was beautifully suited to my temperament. Although the incident had taken place twenty years before I was born, something about World War I has always seemed familiar to me. Perhaps I feel a connection with its old-fashioned Englishness and its sense of deprivation because of my experiences in the harsh, self-conscious English private school I went to in India. And perhaps because my earliest memories are of war—the Japanese occupying our town in northern China in their first successes against the Chinese army, and then later our eleventh-hour voyage from Shanghai to San Francisco a few months before the Japanese attack on Pearl Harbor—I have some sympathy with the surreal ominousness of life in the trenches.

The first thing I did in starting the project was to begin accumulating as much pictorial material on World War I as I could possibly find. I searched new- and used-book stores and told all my friends to be on the lookout for any books on the war that they might find in flea markets or shops outside the city. A lucky break for me was that Michele Kubick, my assistant, went to London on a holiday during this period and brought back invaluable books from antique stores and from the Imperial War Museum. *Life* magazine, of course, had published a series of articles on the war which I was able to locate. I also found a bound collection of the magazine *Illustrated London News* from 1915. I was dealing with the first war in history to have been extensively documented in photographs, and as I poured through my mass of books and magazines and individual photos, I let the light, the texture, and the feeling of the war sink in.

There was a lot of mud in the pictures, and there were horizons that were blasted away to almost nothing. There were men collapsed and near collapse in the decomposing rut of the trench, and men moving quickly but heavily out of the trenches and across the pitted battlefield. Everything was in the process of being obliterated, covered, or turned to the same gray; nevertheless, the surfaces of the landscape and the humans had a kind of confusing fussiness, as though the details were not gone but swollen and distorted by incrustations of mud and fatigue. In a few pictures, the smoke of the explosions or the low, early-morning mist, who knows which, suspended the shattered trees and the moving soldiers in a world without roots or feet, dividing the receding space into two or three flat screens.

It was the spirit of these last photographs that I employed in my first sketches to establish a visual style for the film. I must add here that my experimentation with the style took place slowly, over a period of months, as I worked on both a storyboard to develop the images with which I would tell the story and on the character of those images. By the time I had finished the sample painting, I had (or thought I had) a good idea of how I was going to tell the story. The painting was based on my wanting to use a calligraphic approach to this film. The figures would be built up from a few adroit manipulations of the brush with a minimum of outline and would include only essential details. I also wanted to

1 | World War I photo showing ground fog or gun smoke.

2 | Painting I did to show the visual style of the film (later changed), which used smoky atmosphere of photo 1.

3 | Sketch of a trench scene that I decided was not wintry enough.

4 | *(Overleaf)* The first painting in the film, with the research photo (inset) from which it was derived.

1

2

3

December 25, 1914

5 | Pencil drawings used as basis for finished painting of periscope scene.

6, 7 | Research photos.

8 | Painting of periscope scene.

5

float the figures in ground fog, just as I had seen in the photos, to give the film a dreamlike quality. I had not yet decided exactly how much actual animation there was going to be or how much I would depend on other techniques to give the film movement.

Although I liked the painting, which I showed to Bob Blechman, after a few more weeks of working on the storyboard I realized that the style of this painting was too ethereal for the way I really wanted to tell the story in my film. The more I thought about the letter and how it could be visualized, the more I wanted to evoke the gritty reality that was so evident in the photographs of the war. After all, it wasn't a dream. I was also beginning to understand how complex, difficult, and fascinating it was to develop and refine the storyboard. By the time I made the drawings for the pencil test (which is an actual film made from the pencil drawings), very little in my original storyboard had remained unchanged, and after the pencil test I saw that certain sections didn't work and had to be done differently.

Throughout this early period of working on the film I not only honed and refined the storyboard, but also met with a number of experts. Most notable was Jeffrey Gattral, an animator who advised me on how to achieve certain effects and who made the actual computations for the camera moves. I also conferred with the composer for the sound track, Arnold Black, since I had some ideas for the sound effects and music which I hoped he could incorporate into his score. At this stage Blechman and I were discussing the kind of voice we wanted for the narration. We initially tried a very good professional actor, but ended up using David Jones, one of the musicians we had already engaged for the soldiers' songs. I was not used to working with and depending on so many other people, but aside from the fact that work in film unavoidably involves many people, something strong came out of it for me in terms of my storyboard.

Once I had decided the sample painting was not right, I painted another sketch of a long horizontal view of the inside of a trench. It had some good figures in it, and the color was interesting, but the sketch didn't really look like France in bitter midwinter. I looked at my photographs some more and realized that the winter light in them was soft and diffuse because the skies were so often overcast. My trench painting, on the other hand, was full of the sharp-edged daubs of watercolor that are typical of my way of working and suggest sunlight falling on the forms and casting clearly shaped windows. My soldiers could have been as easily in Tunisia as in France.

I experimented with various strokes and finally came up with an answer. I found that if instead of trying to fade out the wash with a brush freshly dipped in water, which made an abrupt transition, I used a brush that had been partially dried out on a damp cloth, I could soften the edge of a shadow fairly smoothly. Now I had a way to make the soft, rounded shadows of winter. It may sound like a simple thing, but it made a major difference both in how I saw the figures and in the experience of making the paintings. Evoking the somber heaviness of the soldiers' uniforms became a large part of the film's quality for me. Now things were beginning to fall into place: I had a feeling for the light and the forms, which focused my attitude about the subject, and the storyboard itself felt solid and workable. Among Blechman, Gattral, and myself, we had worked out the way the film should move and how to accomplish it.

Basically, the film uses three techniques: camera moves on flat stationary art; separate foreground, middleground, and back-

6   7

90

December 25, 1914

9

10

11

12

13

14

15

16

17

18

19

ground levels that move past each other in one direction or another; and figures, cut out in silhouette, that move across backgrounds. The first technique sometimes involves simple pans,
but in other instances, it means complicated moves, such as spir-
als, across large paintings containing many separate figures or
details. The largest of these paintings, of a tabletop with framed
photographs, measures 30″ x 38″ (76 x 97 cm), and is the biggest
watercolor I have ever done. The second technique typically involves the sky, the distant battlefield, the trench wall, and the
foreground figures as different levels that move. In the third
technique, which comes the closest to standard animation, an action such as walking across the battlefield is broken down into
simple successive steps. I accomplished this by drawing and
painting the figures on thin, stretched watercolor paper, and
when they were dry, I cut them out in silhouette and pasted onto
transparent cels. In this way they could be photographed against
backgrounds or behind partial foregrounds. Most of the transitions in the movie were made as dissolves, or gradual fades from
one image to another. All the art was done on watercolor paper
with the exception of barbed wire and some very tiny, distant
figures; these were drawn directly onto the cel sheets that, in
many cases, backed up the paper art. The planning of the art so
that it could be sized, positioned, and matched for the camera
kept Jeffrey Gattral busy for over two months.

The work on the film progressed rather jerkily for a year and a
half. The project was originally meant to be finished in ten
months, but since none of the artists could make that deadline,
the film was postponed for showing the next year. In my case, the
postponement meant a frantic last six months of work even to
meet the new deadline. For one thing, my paintings were large
and elaborate. I had started with the conviction that making
good paintings for an animated film was not a waste of time, and
I was determined to prove my theory by making the images as
rich and as detailed as I would for any other work. I believed that
since the film was to be animated by the relatively slower dis-
solve method, there would be time for the viewer to take in and
enjoy the quality of the images. I anticipated that the rounded
heaviness I was giving the figures would particularly pay off in
the effect of the film, and so I tried to make them as well drawn
and solidly painted as I could.

As I became more deeply involved in making the paintings, I
found that I needed to take my own research photos to give me
information for specific actions in the story line. I hired a variety
of models for this, dressing them up in heavy army-surplus
clothes in the heat of mid-summer and using the sandy fields of
Long Island as the battleground. I was guided in my photo ses-
sions by Jeffrey Gattral's drawings of how a particular action can
best be broken down for animation. Since I was not attempting
anything approaching full animation, the photographic breakdown of an action never had more than five or six stages. Jeffrey
and I agreed it would have been jarring to see some fast-paced
motion in the midst of a basically dissolve-animation film.

Considering the fact that there was not time or money to re-
shoot any of the scenes or reconsider any of our decisions after
we saw the first print of the film, I am very satisfied with the way
it turned out. I was particularly pleased when Red Grooms, an
artist I admire greatly, said to me that what he really liked about
the film was how heavy everything looked in it. It is probably the
only example of my work about which he could say this, but it
was, I thought, a perceptive reaction.

21

Lake

1977–1980
CBS Records
AD: Paula Scher

1 | This shot of a kitchen sink over-flowing contained the critical element of the curious cat.

2 | A photo I took of water pouring over the lip of a plastic tub. The pouring water in my first shots had been almost invisible.

3 | A pencil sketch from one of my photos, using a square format for the scene; I changed elements of it for the final painting.

4 | The finished album cover.

One aspect of taking my own research photographs that I really like is that often, in the process of taking the photograph, something unexpectedly good will happen. When I am using a model, that person frequently will add a unique idea or character to the picture, and sometimes even without a model an unanticipated quality will emerge from the photo session. In taking my research shots for the first of my Lake album covers, for instance, I ended up with a photo that included a surprise element that changed the effect of that image and the ideas for the subsequent covers.

To backtrack a little: Paula Scher, an art director at Columbia Records with whom I have done a great deal of work, asked me to do a series of jackets for Lake, a German rock group. She had an idea for the first one she wanted me to tackle—she thought it would be funny, and hopefully effective, to do a picture of a sink overflowing as a pictorial pun on the word *lake*. At first I was resistant to the idea, since it immediately summoned up a slick kind of illustration—a tour de force airbrush rendering with every drop of water highlighted. This is a kind of painting outside the technical range of my watercolor style and certainly outside my own esthetic interest. After Paula insisted that in her mind's eye she could already see the image as a McMullan watercolor, I felt obliged to add overflowing kitchen sinks to my creative vision of the world. Maybe the sink didn't have to have quite so many highlights after all.

I decided that, rather than trying to piece together an idealized image of a sink and fake the water overflowing, I would tackle it as if it were a reporting job and paint a specific sink with real water overflowing. My assistant graciously offered to let me use the sink of her old-style New York kitchen for my research photos. It was a round-rimmed porcelain sink that seemed ideal for creating a waterfall edge, and both the sink and the immediate environs looked homey and nostalgic. Michele and I chose particular dishes to be soaking in the sink, lined the floor under the sink with towels and newspapers, placed various bottles and objects strategically, and after setting up the camera on a tripod and pouring a lot of detergent into the sink, turned on the spigots full blast. As the hard stream of tap water beat the soap into iridescent mounds, and suds and water began to slip over the edge, a surprise element popped into the picture. Michele's cat, Smith, jumped up onto the counter next to the sink and began to watch the soapy Niagara and the mess it was making on the floor. This made the whole idea come alive, and I clicked off as many shots as I could. As he circled the sink, the cat was a curious, puzzled participant who gave the scene a drama and a focus that it had been missing. In fact, it was the presence of the cat that made the whole thing into a domestic scene; without Smith, it would have been just a flat portrait of a sink.

When I got the photos back, I decided to use one with Smith standing in the left foreground looking down at the mess on the floor. It gave the picture more depth than the shot of Smith standing on the back rim of the sink, and I liked the way the cat's gaze dramatized the unseen lake. The one problem that I had with the photos was that the water falling over the face of the sink cabinet was almost invisible. Later, back at the studio, I had to take some more shots of water falling over an edge in order to get enough information to develop a way of showing the cascading sheet of water in the painting.

Since Paula Scher had asked me to design a format for the album that would work for future covers for the group, my first

1

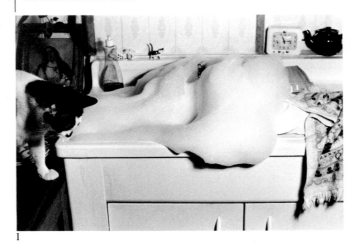

2

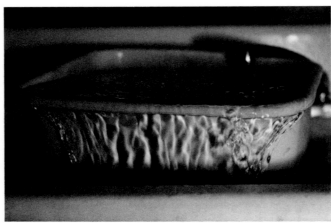

3

sketches were of different shapes that I might use to frame the scenes. Because each of the albums would show a scene illustrating a different pun on the word *lake*, I wanted to use the same framing device on all of the albums to give the series an identity. I decided to contain the major image within a circle and floated this circle more or less in the middle of the square album against a background textured with something appropriate; in the case of this album, the background was droplets of water. Also for this first album I took the existing Lake logo, which was an undistinguished script, and painted it in droplets. For the second and subsequent albums I redesigned the word in my own droplet script, which became the new logo for the group.

Paula liked my sketch a great deal, but it ran into trouble with the product and advertising people at Columbia Records. They felt, according to Paula's account, that this was a very curious and un-hip way to package rock music. To these people, watercolor looked old-fashioned and vaguely effete—how could it stand up on the racks to the socko effects of airbrush or photography? they asked. The fight about using this art went on for weeks with Paula occasionally giving me some hint of the resistance she was meeting. Our side finally won through Paula's sheer perseverance and the intervention of the group's powerful producer, Jimmy Guercio, who happened to like the art.

Now that the sketch was approved, I could begin the actual painting. As several weeks had passed, I found it a struggle to keep the original idea fresh. In any painting where the information itself is difficult to establish—like cascading water and soap bubbles, for example—it is easy for a painting to lapse into rendering. I try, in cases like this, to concentrate on the quality of the brushstrokes as much as on the effects of realism. This amounts to keeping the marks as large as they can be under the circumstances, and as fluid and vigorous in shape as I can make them. I built the soap bubbles up, for instance, not only with a warm gray-purple tone, but also with small, light dabs of pink and blue wash that I hoped might give the suds an iridescence and establish a globular texture that would be different from the elongated shapes of the water.

The first Lake cover attracted a moderate amount of attention when it was released, probably for the same reason that it had been resisted by the product managers of Columbia—it *was* unusual to see rock music being represented in a medium that a great many people associate with civilized English landscapes. Since then, besides the covers for Lake, I have done several other rock and jazz covers, and so the first Lake cover was something of a door opener.

When the second Lake cover assignment came along, the accidental cat became the necessary animal. Paula had been so delighted with the addition of the cat to her original overflowing sink idea that she asked me to incorporate an animal into all the subsequent covers. At first she thought it should always be the same cat, but I argued for the novelty of different animals, thinking to myself that I would certainly like to include my wife's African gray parrot, Ogden Gnash, in the series.

After convincing Paula that a parrot should be the next Lake cover animal, I let ideas for an Ogden album jacket percolate in the back of my mind for a week or so. Then I remembered an incident involving the parrot and a lake of sorts, which had occurred in Sag Harbor, where we have a house on the water. We were sitting on our high deck, which overlooks a cove, and Ogden was with us, perched happily on a vine, nibbling leaves. He

is an entertaining companion because he has a small repertoire of random phrases such as "Are you cold?" "Annie [the cat], come here!" and "Go inside!" which he interjects into the conversation from time to time. Because his wings are clipped in such a way that he can't really fly, we're not afraid of losing him to the great outdoors. But something on this particular day must have startled him, for he suddenly shrieked, flapped his wings wildly, and took off in a long, descending trajectory for the waters of the cove. He had hardly plopped down before Katy, the vigilant mother, raced from the house, down the slope, and into the water to save him. She swam out, and as she reached the struggling bird, she extended her arm, which he gratefully climbed. When he had settled as high as he could on her shoulder, he gave her ear an affectionate peck and said, "It's all right."

As I thought about the album cover, this event became somehow transformed in my mind, and I imagined Ogden standing on Katy's bent knees in the bathtub. The parrot's devotion to Katy would make it possible for me to get such a shot, although I knew that Og would hate every second of it.

The shots I took of Ogden shifting around uneasily on the steep hill formed by Katy's bent legs have some of the terrified but totally focused quality that I imagine he exuded as Katy swam up to him in the cove. He cocks his head slightly as if to register more clearly the next catastrophe that is to befall him. The photographs turned out very much as I had imagined the scene—simple forms that could be adjusted to make a strong composition, and a very real and animated portrait of the parrot.

When I began the sketch, I decided to paint the bathroom in that obnoxious shade of pink that tiles often come in. It amused me to do a "too pink" painting, and I also thought it was a nice way to complement the parrot's one area of bright color, his pure red tail feathers.

The sketch was approved, with one change—Paula wanted the water in the tub to be overflowing in order to give the picture more action and suggest another aspect of the word *lake*. In my final picture, I enjoyed the pristine quality of the image—the detailed texture of Ogden and the sharp edges in the painting of the tiles. I also felt that in this cover the droplets were evoked more subtly and created a more elegant design than they had in the first cover. I was also pleased to have conjured up the personality of Ogden, the parrot, and to have made a modest start on what I hope will be a lifelong study of my wife, Katy.

The most recent album in the Lake series is one that Paula decided to call *Ouch!* and for which she again suggested an image. Why not show a dog being scalded by an exploding radiator? she asked. If I was a truly good and caring person, I suppose I would have been horrified by the cruelty of her idea and rejected it out of hand, but as it was, I only questioned the element of the bursting radiator. Couldn't we find something else to scald the dog with? It would be impossible to convincingly fake just how a radiator would look as it exploded, I explained. I told her that I would think about the problem and get back to her with a solution. In a few days I had thought of an answer that was suggested to me when I noticed how much our cats are underfoot when my wife and I are cooking. Why couldn't the dog be under the line of fire from a pot lid dripping a scalding stream of water as a housewife thoughtlessly holds it aloft while checking the pasta on the stove? Although it was a little Rube Goldbergian as an idea, I was sufficiently convinced it would work to go ahead with taking some research photos. And did I have a dog model in mind for

5,6 | Two photographs of Ogden the parrot sitting on my wife's knees.
7 | The color sketch.
8 | The finished album jacket.

5

6

7

8

the job! A country neighbor's black-and-white mongrel runt—which protects his territory with paranoid ferocity and an unfortunate tinny yapping—struck me as born for the part of the scaldee. The neighbor graciously agreed to lend his dog for this kind of stardom, and I enlisted the help of his son as the animal trainer. We set about trying to make the dog look pained for the photograph by banging pot lids together. It turned out to be not too difficult, since the range of the dog's emotions went straight from aggression to cowering submission, and I was able to use one of the variations on the latter expression as the basis for my hapless dog. With a photograph of my wife unwillingly playing the role of the thoughtless cook, I proceeded to do the pencil sketch to show Paula. She liked it.

Because the image was so chock-full of action—twisting dog, outstretched arm, and billowing clouds of steam—I decided that I should use a fairly broad but clear drawing to start with. I saw it as almost a cartoon explanation of what was going on, and so I used strong lines and bright colors as I put down my first painted strokes. In this case I didn't want my drawing to disappear completely as I added the subsequent washes of color. The painting of the steam took some careful use of very light washes, but I tried to attack the rest of the painting with bravura and courage in the color. It was not a painting that looked particularly beautiful at every stage of its creation, and at times I wondered if it wasn't turning into a heavy mess, but finally it came together as an image with the strong, crazy quality I had hoped for.

My attempts in all of the Lake covers, and particularly in *Ouch!*, to illustrate fairly complex subjects in a clear way while maintaining a quality of immediacy in the painting are a good example of the balancing act I must do in a great deal of my work. While I am trying to convince the viewer that a kitchen sink is overflowing or a dog is being scalded, I am also trying to evoke that reality through a vocabulary of lines, marks, and daubs that are natural to me and which are essentially abstract. When I am succeeding, there is a flow to the activity and an intuitive relationship among all the parts of the painting that is coherent to me; when I am not succeeding, my logical, less intuitive thinking starts to take over and I make separate, discrete decisions that erode my sense of the whole work. Although every picture needs logic, particularly in the planning stages where the mind must absorb new information, the act of painting eventually becomes a game ruled by emotions, psychic reflexes, sensual responses to the materials, and an intuitive relationship to the subject matter.

Often what I am trying to avoid in the case of a difficult informational assignment like the Lake albums, is rendering the subject rather than painting it. The distinction is somewhat hard to describe, but when I lapse into rendering, it feels as if all my energy were going into the simulation of the physical subject matter—a desperate and single-minded effort to convince the viewer that a form turns in such and such a way. When I am in this track, I usually resort to physical manipulations that have no pleasure for me—laborious layers of wash or tiny strokes piled up on top of one another. I lose my sense of simultaneously evoking a form and playing a game with brushstrokes and watercolor washes that is also satisfying on an esthetic level. I don't mean to suggest that when this game is working (that is, when I have avoided rendering), I can see my brushstrokes totally independently of the subject matter, for that is not the case. My perception is always that the brushstroke is connected to the information, but my delight is that it continues to be an interesting brushstroke.

9

10

11

Baader-Meinhof

July 18, 1978
Esquire
AD: Milton Glaser

Sometimes when I am sitting at my drawing table thinking of ideas for a particular assignment, it occurs to me that the total range of my metaphoric invention is circumscribed by a tiny list of events and images that caught my attention between the ages of five and twenty-five. It is disappointing to believe that I became a closed system in my middle twenties; but I think that in terms of archetypal incidents and objects, nothing very strong has been added to my subconscious vault since that time. I have, for instance, made pictures about the Vietnam war, but for me, images of that war will never be as evocative as the World War I pictures I once saw in a book that showed soldiers in the trenches of France—or my own World War II memories of being aboard a freighter in the Indian Ocean preparing to abandon our ship, which we thought was about to be bombed. In mentioning the last incident, I do not mean to suggest that only those events in my life which were truly dramatic have been added to the primal storehouse of my mind. If one could visualize this area of my brain as a room filled with objects, it would contain as much trivia—scenes from Tarzan movies, terrible eyeglass frames I once wore, and pages from Phantom comics—as it would hold important objects representing really tragic or magnificent moments in my life.

I could find no better specimen from this mental junk shop than what I dug up for an assignment for *Esquire* on the Baader Meinhof terrorist gang in Germany. When I read the manuscript by Jon Bradshaw, which described the details of how Andreas Baader, the imprisoned gang leader, and four accomplices engineered an escape from a room in a heavily guarded library, my mind sped back over the years to a diagram I had seen in *True Detective* magazine. The diagram showed where Lana Turner's lover, Johnny Stompanato, had been stabbed in her bedroom and where his body had fallen. With a series of crude drawings and dotted lines, it also showed the subsequent movements of Lana and her daughter Cheryl in the room. The drawing was a cutaway view that let you see into the room as though you were a child playing with a dollhouse, with all of the walls intact but the roof removed. I recall looking at the drawing for a long time thinking about what had gone on, particularly all the parts of the story that I was convinced were being left out by the magazine.

This was neither the first nor the last crime chart I had ever seen, but its strong effect on my imagination reveals how powerful these drawings were for me. Now, twenty to thirty years later, I was connecting them to a story for *Esquire*. Since the central drama of the piece was in the logistics of the escape, what better way to show these movements than with a "mechanical" drawing? There were enough details in the Baader Meinhof manuscript to provide the basis for a "police diagram" painting, which might do for the *Esquire* reader what the Lana Turner/Stompanato art had done for me. My painting was to be in color and would describe more details of the interior and of the people than the *True Detective* diagram, of course, but I wanted it to satisfy that same curiosity about exactly where each person had stood and where each had moved at the decisive moment of the escape.

I found a library at Pratt Institute that provided a balcony from which I could photograph at the right angle, and several students who were willing to play terrorists. Later, in painting the picture, I was able to put to good use those exploratory lines that so often occur in my work. Here they became part of the sense of movement and of general nervousness in the picture.

1

2

3

7

8

4

5

6

9

Illustrators 20

1978
Society of Illustrators
AD: Doug Johnson

1 | Pencil sketch, showing newsstand idea, that I did before I took research photos.
2 | One of twenty Polaroid photographs I took of a local newsstand.
3 | The photo I decided to use.
4 | Pencil design based on photo 3.
5 | The color sketch that was shown for approval.
6 | A second sketch I did for myself to improve the color and the design.

The context of an illustration inevitably colors the effect of the idea within that illustration. Encountering a theatrical poster as a huge, colorful design within the dank grayness of the subway, for instance, is a different experience from seeing that same image within the glossy pages of a magazine. Our expectations about how certain subjects should be dealt with are also part of the context of a graphic image. To see a poster for an adventure movie treated with the same restraint and delicacy as a perfume ad would be surprising (but could be effective). I try to recognize the context of each assignment I do and to use this knowledge to increase the impact of that particular illustration. Sometimes I work with the context, fulfilling its expectations in the same way Woody Allen might choose to do a genre romance movie, and sometimes I work against those expectations to gain as much drama as I can through the element of surprise.

When I began to work on an image for the twentieth annual Society of Illustrators exhibition poster, there were contextual elements that I felt would affect the way my poster would be seen. One was the nature of the society itself, and the posters created for it in the preceding years. I also thought that I should consider the audience of illustrators who would see it.

In considering the nature of the society, I recognized that beyond the usual conservative drift of most professional associations, the Society of Illustrators also has the extra historical pull of illustration's "Golden Age"—that period in the thirties and forties when illustration was a much more visible and highly paid activity. This aura of having belonged to a different and better time has touched many of the society's posters in the last decade. Several have had historical themes, and those not about the past have had topics such as magic, the circus, or mythology. These last subjects seem to suggest that the illustrator's world is a dreamlike realm not strongly connected to the reality we see on the six o'clock TV news. There may be some truth to the idea that the illustrator frequently deals with time past or a romantic view of the present, but since my own bias is toward using the grittiness of real life, I thought it would be interesting and provocative to do a poster unlike the past posters for the society. I decided to choose a very contemporary and unromantic subject.

The exhibition I was asked to announce was the twentieth, and Doug Johnson, who was the show's chairman and who had asked me to do the poster, suggested that I might express the number as a roman numeral. I couldn't seem to do anything with the number itself, and so I went on to thinking about a general image. What floated into my head at this point was a newsstand. I liked the fact that a newsstand is a street gallery for an illustrator's work, that unpretentious point where one's private midnight labors finally meet the public.

While I was sketching possible stagings and inhabitants for my newsstand, I also thought about adding some element that would be directed specifically to my audience of fellow illustrators. I wanted to include something in the poster that had to do with making a picture, some fragment of the process of illustrating that my audience would not expect to see but nevertheless would understand and respond to as they might to a private joke. I thought of the test brushstrokes an artist makes on a scrap of paper to twist the brush into its sharpest point or remove excess pigment. By including this element, which goes against all standards of neatness and "finish," I wanted to give a little shock, of course—but at the same time, I had always been impressed by how beautiful these patches of brushstrokes could be. In my de-

1

2

3

4

5

6

sign for the poster, I saw them as irregular abstract columns of color and texture flanking an articulated central image.

Now that I had my basic ideas for the design, it was time to take some specific reference photographs, and so on the next Sunday morning, I set out for the local newsstand. I decided to use my somewhat clumsy 4 x 5 camera with a Polaroid back rather than a 35mm camera. Besides the fact that I could see what I was getting right away, I felt that my increased presence with the tripod might create an interesting human chemistry—or maybe I just wanted to play street photographer. At any rate, I asked the vendor's permission, set myself up in the street facing the newsstand, and started photographing. Every few minutes, I would have to hurriedly grab my spindly equipment and move it out of the path of an oncoming car, but I managed to get some shots. The sort of images I got certainly had the feeling of everyday life—they were banal and, except for the occasional cute dog, bereft of dramatic incident. Someone else might have been discouraged, but I knew that somewhere in these anonymous tableaux there was a good poster. I went back to the studio with about fifteen photographs, and after studying them and making some drawings, I decided that one shot I had taken, of a young couple walking hand in hand, had the secret ingredient. The two people were clearly contemporary, they walked with a strong rhythm, and I liked the complete attention they gave to the newsstand. The photograph was dark, difficult to decipher, and not filled with the kind of light I usually use to define form. Still, the picture had a candid spirit that appealed to me, and I proceeded with a sketch.

It is a tribute to Doug Johnson's persuasiveness (and confidence in me), that he was able to sell my concept for the poster to the society's board with only my first sketch. As soon as I got it back from him, I realized it was fussy, overworked, dirty-colored and badly designed. I had not invented a light or color scheme that worked to replace the darkness of the photograph, and my paint strokes on the side had become boring, evenly proportioned pillars instead of the slashes and jabs I had first imagined. The lettering peeked coyly out of the composition on an angle that had nothing to do with anything else. I had obviously chosen to do the sketch on a "stiff" day.

With a fresh eye, I embarked on a new sketch for myself. This one was much better; it was filled with an exploratory, iridescent quality that I never quite repeated even in the finish. Much of the effect of this sketch came from leaving the red-outlined figures uncolored, except for their hair. In the sketch they look like either fast-moving lovers or escapees from a lunatic asylum. I liked the aura, but when I tried to paint the couple larger, the power of the effect disappeared. I tried three times to carry out this sketch, but I couldn't recapture the vitality of the original drawing, and so I decided that I would have to make another change in the color and style of the painting. In a fourth sketch, I painted the figures darker against a lighter newsstand and with a precision in the drawing that I knew I could handle on a larger scale. I liked it well enough to embark on a finished painting. The final piece is not exactly like any of the sketches. I made many adjustments as I went along, increasing the complexity and texture of the whole piece and allowing the poster to become flatter in the process. I think it is this flatness that particularly pleases me. The effect hovers between realism and restrained decoration in a way that I had never quite achieved before—nor have I repeated it since.

7

ILLUSTRA

8

9

ANNUAL EXHIBITION
THE SOCIETY OF ILLUSTRATORS
128 EAST 63RD STREET, N.Y.C., MONDAY — FRIDAY 10 A.M.-5 P.M.
EDITORIAL & BOOK, FEBRUARY 8 — MARCH 7, 1978
ADVERTISING, INSTITUTIONAL & TV, MARCH 15 — APRIL 12, 1978

Illustration by James McMullan, Art Direction by Doug Johnson, Design by Anne Leigh/Performing Dogs, Printing by Grinthal Press Inc. N.Y.C., Separation by Computerized Quality Separation N.Y.C., Typography by The Type Group Inc., Printed on Pastelle 80 Text "Natural White" by Strathmore Paper Co.

Paranoia

April 23, 1979
New West magazine
AD: Philip Hays

I was asked to do this cover for *New West* magazine by Phil Hays, who was then a consultant to the magazine. I think that Phil, a very old friend who had shared a few scary experiences with me in New York, took a certain amount of pleasure in assigning this subject to me. When he called from Los Angeles, I could tell he thought something was very funny.

"Jim, we're doing an issue on paranoia, and, for some reason, I thought of you for the cover." He laughed wickedly and continued, "I mean, I doubt if you'll have to spend much time on research." Another chortle. I laughed, too, and after suggesting that no one could do the cover as authoritatively as he, I agreed to do the job for the price of a good alarm system.

Actually, it was an interesting job for me. Now I could try to express the idea of paranoia head on, rather than spooning it into illustrations on other subjects as a kind of psychological sauce, as I had done on several occasions. (See "Portrait of an Aging Hustler" and my covers for the Borges books.)

The challenge in evoking the idea of paranoia, essentially, was to think of a potentially dangerous situation in which it is not clear whether the danger is real or lies in the mind of the subject. The image I came up with was a man seen from the back, at fairly close range, but walking away from the viewer. The man turns his head sharply, as if to discover something behind him, and, indeed, there *is* something behind him, for we see an ominous shadow of a hatted figure cast on the man's back. I also imagined that the scene behind the figure would include a house or some other kind of landscape that would establish the locale as California. It was a simple idea that depended on the expressiveness of the body gesture and the man's face to make it succeed. Phil Hays, himself a consumate illustrator, understood what I was aiming for and gave me the okay to proceed without a sketch.

I was not quite sure what my "paranoid" should look like, but I discussed the cover with a friend who suggested someone to play the part. I met with this man and, although he somehow didn't seem quite right for the role, I set up my camera and took a number of shots.

Besides my vague reservations about the appropriateness of the model's looks for the cover idea, I also had difficulty conveying to him the spirit of the pose I wanted. I had a very specific pose in mind: a tense, almost strained turn of the head that would suggest that the person, unwilling to fully acknowledge his fear by turning around completely to confront the threat, nonetheless tries to see what he thinks is happening by turning his head sharply and looking out of the corner of his eye. I also wanted the man's figure to look like he was moving, and the whole body attitude, although strained, had to be believable.

I had the impression, later confirmed by the developed film, that I had not successfully directed my model to give me the pose I wanted, and so I later asked my wife to take shots of me as the paranoid. As Phil might have predicted, one of these photos did have the right tension in it to use as the basis for the painting.

In doing the actual painting, I was surprised by how interesting it was to establish a shadow lying across the herringbone material of my jacket—much more interesting than it would have been on the plain light material worn by my model. I painted the shadow in several layers, adjusting the color of the pattern within it to give it a warmer glow and to make it look like it really sits on the surface. It is my favorite part of the painting.

1

2

3

4

Loon Lake

1980
The Franklin Library
AD: Joanne Giaquinto

This was the first book illustrating I had done in many years, and I was pleased to have an opportunity to do drawings for a new novel that I particularly liked. The newness of the novel meant that I didn't have to struggle to ignore previous images that had been made to illustrate the book, and the fact that I liked the book meant that I could deal with its spirit and subject matter with enthusiasm.

The novel, *Loon Lake* by E. L. Doctorow, was being printed in a limited first edition by the Franklin Library, and although it was my first Franklin Library book, it was the second time I had illustrated Doctorow's writing. In 1975, *Sports Illustrated* had commissioned me to illustrate an excerpt from his soon-to-be-released novel, *Ragtime*. Like millions of other readers, I was very impressed by Doctorow's book, and as an artist, I was fascinated by the description and development of scenes, which I suspected had begun with his contemplation of famous historical photographs. At the center of certain descriptions in the book, I thought I recognized photographs, like the famous Edward Steichen portrait of J. P. Morgan, around which Doctorow had created psychological and narrative "answers" for the mystery posed by the photograph.

Several years later, when Edgar Doctorow bought a house in Sag Harbor on the same cove as mine, I had a chance to confirm my theory. We were introduced one summer afternoon by a mutual friend who had involved us in a tennis game. I was very pleased that Doctorow remembered my illustrations for *Ragtime* and in the ensuing conversation he said that, yes, certain historical photographs could generate ideas for him.

It was Doctorow who had requested that Franklin Library ask me to illustrate *Loon Lake*. My original positive feelings on accepting the job increased after I read the manuscript. The new novel had the rich language of *Ragtime*, but its story development was less like *Ragtime*'s shifting montage and, despite its use of several voices, more like the emotional and linear novels of the 1930s, the time in which it is set.

After the editor and I discussed the scenes to be illustrated, I proceeded to find models to play the roles for my research photos. The central character, described as "Joe from Paterson," I saw as a man of passionate rebellion who could as easily have been a criminal as a hero. In the story, Joe goes from a resourceful but larcenous adolescence to an adulthood in which he travels as a hobo and a carnival worker, and finally, to a strange connection with an immensely wealthy man. Consequently, I felt Joe needed to have a certain light in his eyes—that of someone who is not crazy, but is willing to go to the edge. I thought of a New York City cop I know whose handsome young face has a look of having been to the edge and seen too much. But he also looks like he can handle himself physically in the decisive way Joe from Paterson handles himself in the book. My friend the cop knew a beautiful young blond who was perfect in looks and, as it turned out, in acting ability, for the part of the heroine. Two of my actor friends played the other four parts I needed.

I painted the illustrations in black and white and tried to give them a solid, realistic style that evokes the 1930s, as well as enough vigorous, calligraphic brush drawing to provide them with a contemporary energy. In the painting of the four figures grouped around the radio, I particularly like the way the drawing goes from the broad description of the man gesturing in the foreground to the intricate delineation of the radio and the wallpaper in the background.

1

2

3

4

5

6

7

8

10

11

12

9

13

The White Album

June 4, 1979
New West magazine
AD: Roger Black

1 | Magazine photo I used as reference for Ramon Novarro figure.
2 | Photo of Paul Robert Ferguson, one of Novarro's killers.
3 | My own photo of a model.
4 | The finished painting of the Novarro scene.
5 | Preliminary sketch for painting 4.

My earliest attempts at illustrating were marked by a quality that bordered on the inscrutable. The obscurity of these first drawings was partly the result of my ambitious interest in illustrating the most difficult aspects of literature. I was attracted, not to stories with clear action for which I might have easily arrived at a coherent visual equivalent, but to writing that was about the elusive and shifting relationships between people. Therefore, it was J. D. Salinger rather than Ernest Hemingway who provided me with texts during my years at art school, and considerations of irony rather than courage that sparked the images I made. In the time since then, I have been unable to entirely quash my love of subtle, psychological writing and the opportunity it provides for creating dense visual metaphors.

An assignment from *New West* magazine to illustrate an excerpt from Joan Didion's *The White Album* was just such an opportunity. Subtitled *A Chronicle of Survival in the Sixties*, Didion's intense diary is narrated in a voice that is both flat and compelling. The events described are like pieces of a shattered mirror, which reflect the narrator's growing sense of horror toward the times in which she finds herself and the disintegration she experiences within her own personality. Besides admiring the tone and subject of her writing, I found her way of telling the story, through acutely observed fragments, an incredible match for the staging and psychology of my work. After reading *The White Album*, I knew I could do interesting illustrations for it.

Because Didion's book was organized like a diary, it struck me that my art might echo the literary form in some way. I knew, certainly, that I would focus on very small moments in the narrative, very much as Didion had focused on the events she had observed. Her writing made no attempt to cover or sum up a whole incident, nor would my drawings. But, beyond that, I thought of a way to dramatize the notative, almost informal visual quality of the illustrations on the page by incorporating lines from the text into the images and letting the shapes of the paintings assume erratic silhouettes rather than rectangles. I also decided to use a painting approach I had been experimenting with: a scribbly brushstroke that seemed to come out of an implicit rhythm or energy that I felt certain subject matter had; when the strokes were piled on top of one another, they formed a very satisfying fat crosshatch texture.

One of the scenes I chose in the text was of an evening that ended with the murder of Ramon Novarro, the silent-screen star, by two young brothers, Paul and Thomas Ferguson, who apparently had operated as hustlers. Didion tells of the event partly through the transcript of the trial, and I chose one line of this dialogue to include in my picture. I wanted to suggest a moment during the evening of the murder when the aspects of sensuality, violence, and absurdity were evenly balanced. When my painting was finished, I was particularly satisfied with the expression on Novarro's face and the way the brushstrokes on the young man's torso seemed both sensual and spikily forbidding.

The excerpt that ran for fifteen pages in the magazine included nine illustrations. Roger Black, the art director, made an effective choice in deciding to run the art as big as possible, in some cases even larger than the original art, thus deriving a great deal of drama from the texture and looseness of the paintings. It was a good example of how the design context can help to reveal the character of illustrations.

1

2

3

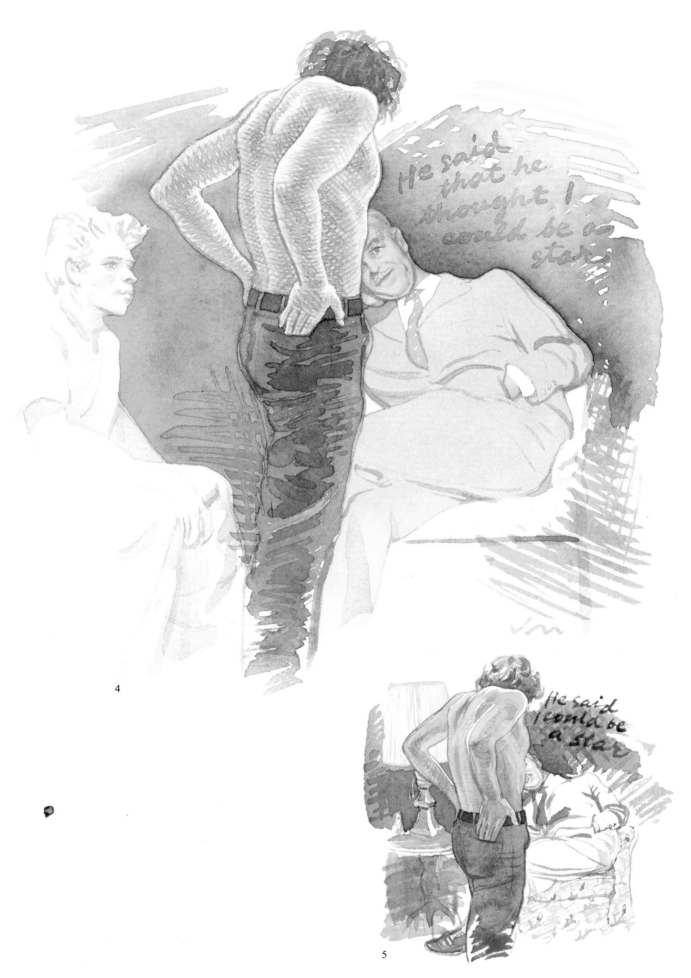

4

5

The White Album

6

7

8

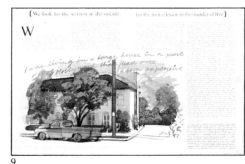

9

I was living in a large house in a part of Hollywood that had once been expensive

10

He smiled at us all and waited for his lawyer, Charles Garry, to set up the tape recorder

11

Borges Covers

1979
E. P. Dutton
AD: Al Manso

When I got out of art school, my portfolio reflected both the experimental stage of my artwork and the influence of various classes. I quickly recognized that if my portfolio was to get me work, I would have to concentrate on one area and do new samples directed to that market. Because I like to read, I decided to do a portfolio of book jackets. One of the first people to give me work was Cyril Nelson of E. P. Dutton, and for a number of my early years as an illustrator, he was a sustaining and supportive client. During this time, I learned a great deal about compressing large subjects into a simple, posterized image, but I gradually drifted away from jacket design and toward magazine illustration, which allows me to indulge my natural interest in the nuances and complexity of information. From time to time, however, I still do jackets for books, and I seem to find it easier now to find metaphors that are both dramatic and natural to me.

This series of jackets for the stories of Jorge Luis Borges was such a project. Twelve years ago Cy had commissioned me to do two other Borges covers, and so he knew that I admired and had a real affinity for Borges's simple but reverberating tales. I connect my own experience with these stories in a way that might not be accurate from the author's point of view, but the associations are useful to me in finding strong imagery and establishing mood. I have no idea whether Borges intends his stories to evoke the particular spirit of the 1930s, but when he writes about events that take place in the saloons and haciendas of Buenos Aires, I can imagine similar intrigues happening on my parents' Tsingtao veranda, in the colonial China of the 1930s. There is enough similarity in the cultivated mannerisms, the sexual liaisons between members of different classes, and the incipient violence of both societies to make this comparison useful to me in imagining the characters of Borges's stories.

My design for *The Aleph*, for instance, went through many stages of surreal imagery but ended up with a head that I modeled after a 1937 magazine advertisement for hats. The man's cool sophistication reminded me of a Borges hero and also of the charming but ruthless men featured in my mother's stories of her tropical flirtations. My first idea for *Chronicles of Bustos Domecq*, the man scribbling in his journal near a statuary head, came from my earliest memories of the stern masters who tried to teach me Latin in a missionary school.

Actually, the series had started not with the *Aleph* jacket but with the image of the parrot. I had originally been asked to design a format and an all-purpose visual for eight Borges books. I came up with the parrot, not because the bird figured in any particular tale but because it seemed a good way to establish the South American locale of the stories, and the silhouette conveyed the feeling of mystery in the writing. Dutton liked the parrot but decided that each collection of stories should have its own image. I used the parrot on the book for which it seemed most appropriate, *Doctor Brodie's Report* (which takes place deep in the jungle), and went on to find visual symbols for the rest of the books. I also used the red border and fusions of bright color in each jacket to identify it as part of the series. I felt very free in finding metaphors for these books, as I knew the connection I was making was one of spirit and not of fact. I was also very comfortable with the mood of exotic malevolence I had set up for the series. Because I had been playful in my creative choices rather than agonizing over them, the jackets are a satisfying and seamless mixture of design, realism, and psychology.

1

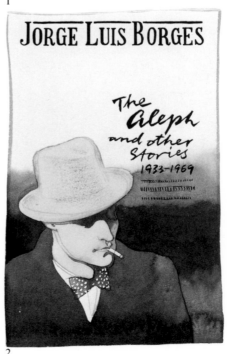

2

6

Doctor Brodie's Report
3

Chronicles of Bustos Domecq
7

4

5

JORGE LUIS BORGES

A Universal History of Infamy
8

JORGE LUIS BORGES

The Book of Sand
9

Retrospective Poster

1979
Visual Arts Museum
AD: Richard Wilde/Ayelet Bender

1–8 | Various poses I tried out for the portrait research on this poster.
9 | Sketch, based on Polaroid, using a large calligraphic signature.
10 | Sketch, based on Polaroid, including tough-guy characters as blob shapes.
11 | Sketch, also based on Polaroid, using abstract paint strokes and linear tough guys.

When Silas Rhodes, president of the School of Visual Arts, invited me to have a one-man show at the school's museum, I was very pleased and honored. Because of my long and special connection to the school, it was particularly gratifying to be able to celebrate my career within its walls. My association with the school started eight years ago when Silas Rhodes invited me to teach a course in which I could experiment with my own ideas about teaching illustration. The experience of developing this course and of meeting the many students I have had continues to be one of the best things that has happened to me.

My problem (if doing a poster for one's own retrospective can be called a problem) was to settle on one image that would in some way evoke the spirit of my work. Given that the exhibition would show illustrations from a twenty-year career and follow my art as I evolved though big changes in my life, I was resigned to the fact that the poster could not hope to recapitulate the whole show. It could only work if it limited itself to one dramatic, but central, issue.

As I let my mind wander over the terrain of possibilities, I came up with several subjects and ideas that occurred frequently enough in my work to be important. I could remember a lot of water-related pictures, for instance, as well as a period dominated by maps and grids; an idealized landscape pops up on a regular basis, as do shadow ideas, and the shadowy world of crime. None of these reveries got me very far in finding a concrete image for the poster, however. They all seemed too abstract as starting points. Only my repeated connection to criminal subject matter struck me as at all promising. Once I had focused on this area my mind quickly jumped to a specific image: tough guys. I have drawn a lot of tough guys in my time, and many of those illustrations have either been particularly popular in the world or important to me. Certainly my painting of the two men in the Brooklyn disco series is the one image people remember best from my most publicized project. Other "golden toughies" include the truck driver I painted for the *New York Times*, my illustration of an aging hustler for the cover of *New York* magazine, and the Baader Meinhof terrorists I did for *Esquire*.

I had a flash of how amusing it would be to make a painting about me confronting the tough guys. The scenario might somehow suggest that they had all come back from the big illustration in the sky to give me trouble, or at least to haunt me a little. I have to explain at this point that the humor of the image would come out of the fact that I myself am *not* a tough guy. Depending on the source, I would probably be characterized as a regular guy, strangely intense, or a professorial type. I am not happy with any of these descriptions, but I have learned to live with their rough accuracy. I could see that this idea would be interesting not only because of the clear demarcation of roles, but also as an existential exercise in portraying myself as the ultra-refined artist facing the hostile barbarians of my imagination.

On a philosophical level, the confrontation between the tough man and myself is an allegory for my feelings about survival. Despite the middle-class circumstances of my childhood and the advantages my talent has given me, I have never entirely rid myself of the feeling that my life is a difficult feat of "hanging on." I have felt that each successive stage of my life has been endured against the forces of chaos both inside and outside myself. But because the desperateness of these feelings has slowly subsided over the years and I find myself alive, relatively happy and healthy, and in some kind of accommodation with the furtive

1–8

120

9

10

11

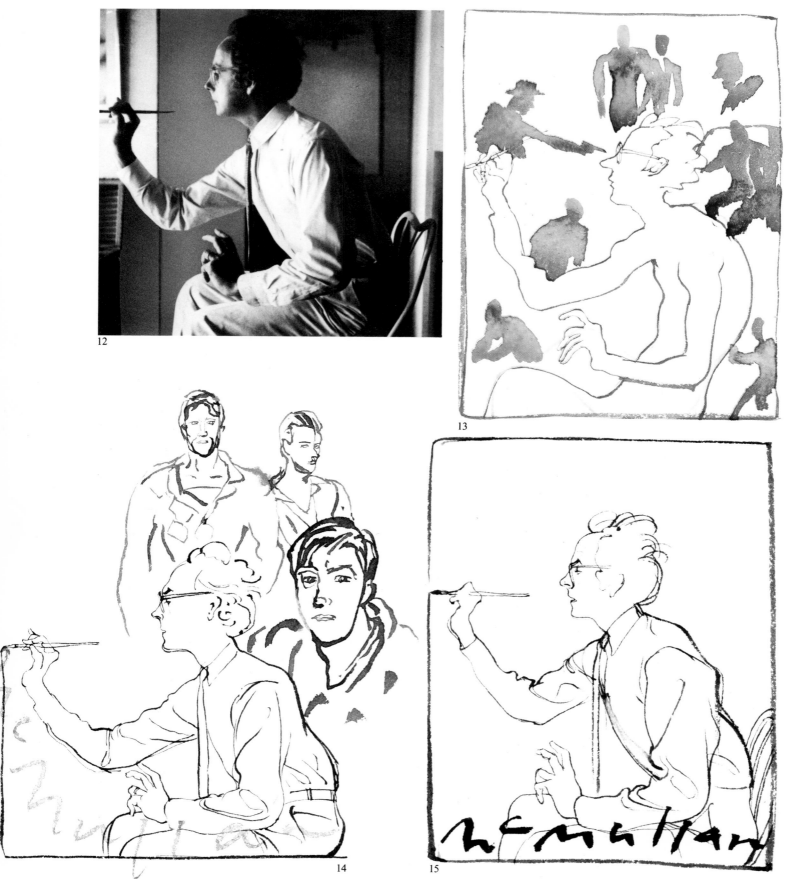

12

13

14

15

12   Polaroid photo that I finally settled on as my research.

13   Cartoony sketch that helped me see the characterization that might work.

14, 15   Two more "correct" drawings made from photo 12.

16   Sketch exploring a rougher manner of painting background figures.

17   In this painting, which almost became the finish, I achieved the elegant drawing I thought I wanted.

16

17

Retrospective Poster

fourteen-year-old boy still trapped inside me, the idea for the poster—me facing the tough guys—is a celebration of sheer perseverance.

After deciding that my poster image would be a portrait of me as prim esthete in some way surrounded or challenged by the macho denizens of my illustrations, I had my wife take photographs of me in a variety of poses, delicately holding a watercolor brush. As you can see from the first three sketches, I tried using the figures from several past illustrations as a frame or as floating patches around the front-facing image of myself. Although the portrait in sketch 9 is fascinating in a ravaged way, the effect of all these sketches is too static and the elements too disconnected. Besides wanting a more dynamic shape in the poster and more satisfyingly connected elements, I also felt that the characterization of myself was verging on the morbid. I was aiming for the dandy as played by Leslie Howard, but what I was getting was Vincent Price.

It occurred to me that if I did the portrait of myself in profile, I might get the same clear body language and stylization I had achieved with the laughing comic in the *Comedians* poster, and the more complicated shape of the side-view figure might increase the vitality of this poster. When I posed for the side-view photo, I emphasized the spirit of my movement so that it would be theatrical and obvious. The body itself became a quickly understood gesture, like the movements of a mime or a dancer.

In sketches 13 through 17, I was working toward a portrait done in an open, elegant, linear way and surrounded by characters from previous illustrations painted in a darker, broader, and more textural style. The contrast of the two styles, I hoped, would help to articulate the contrast between me and the tough guys. I liked the drawing of myself, but I couldn't resolve the esthetic connection between the portrait and the characters around it. They looked as if I had just stuck them around the portrait or had meant them to occupy a real space, beyond the large figure, in which they might suddenly turn and begin to fight each other.

As far as I can remember, I came upon the very opposite idea—making the portrait a washy silhouette—simply by chance. I was doodling away with the brush and I happened to make a small, solidly painted version of the self-portrait. The idea clicked immediately, and I knew that this approach to the central figure would give me a solid armature upon which to build the rest of the elements and that, furthermore, the depersonalization of the portrait through silhouetting was better for the spirit of the poster. It made me more of an abstraction of a character and therefore funnier as an archetype.

Having had so much difficulty in integrating the tough guys as excerpted elements from previous illustrations, I decided to take a more straightforward approach. I divided up the space behind my back into rectangles and painted in versions of the whole illustration from which each of the characters had come. This arrangement suggested both that the pictures were part of my past (behind me) and that I carried them on my back (a treasury of good works? a burden? a penance?).

Ah, yes! What about the gunman in front of me? He had evolved at some earlier stage of the game from a small figure in an illustration I had done about the mafia (one that is not in this book), and I had liked the invention of connecting him up to a zigzag brushstroke as if he were a jack-in-the-box springing from my brush. What does he mean? Maybe that nothing is ever settled or that I need a lot of tension to be creative or that the little people are now armed and dangerous.

18

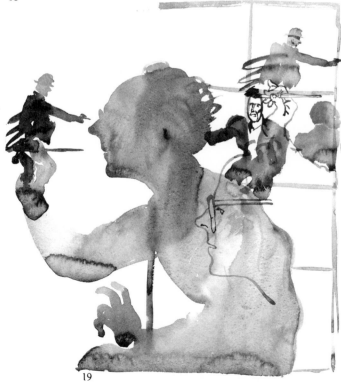

19

JAMES McMULLAN RETROSPECTIVE · NOVEMBER 29TH–DECEMBER 19TH

YOU ARE CORDIALLY INVITED TO THE OPENING ON THURSDAY, NOVEMBER 29TH, FROM 5:30-7:30 PM. THE VISUAL ARTS MUSEUM, 209 EAST 23RD STREET, NEW YORK CITY 10010. MONDAY THROUGH THURSDAY, NOON TO 9:00 PM, FRIDAY, 11:00 AM TO 4:30 PM. CLOSED WEEKENDS.

Poco

1979
CBS Records
AD: Paula Scher

Sometimes an assignment will come along which seems like an inevitable subject for me. When Paula Scher of Columbia Records asked me to do paintings of western scenes for the covers of two albums by the rock group Poco, my first thought was "Cowboys, of course! Why has it taken me so long to getting around to painting cowboys?" Actually, about twelve years ago, I did sixteen pages of drawings in *Life* magazine for a story by Mark Twain on the American West. I drew cowboys stranded in a flood, roping calves, being scalped, and riding off into the sunset. As terrific as I thought these illustrations were, they did not start a stampede of art directors into my studio asking for more. Paula's assignment was the first one since then, and she had no particular instructions about the kind of scene she wanted other than that it should be appropriate for the romantic, western-inspired rock songs of Poco.

Perhaps I shouldn't have been surprised that with the challenge of this very free assignment, I clutched up a little before I found the way I wanted to do the paintings. For one thing, deciding on how to approach painting a cowboy picture was not as simple as I had first thought. What I encountered in myself and in my research was that the subject of cowboys had become obscured by so many different layers of romance that, like a repeatedly and badly painted room, it had to be scraped down before I could see its original character.

The degree to which the idea of the cowboy had become encrusted with illusion was brought home to me by the fact that in the first three places I looked for research, I found the files fat with magazine clippings of Marlboro cigarette ads. The photographs in these ads are beautifully staged and detailed and, as advertising psychology, probably brilliant. But the lie they perpetrate, that a group of men engaged in the historical vocation of the cowboy remains unchanged to our times, bothered me. It diluted the meaning and reality of a way of life that must have existed very differently. I thought that if the idea of cowboys is really summed up in the smug self-confidence of these cigarette ads, then it's going to be very hard to make a western picture that is about anything more than a particular kind of clothing and a strong jaw. Because cowboy imagery has been used so much in our time, for selling everything from cigarettes to cologne and for merchandising expensive pointed-toe boots, I realized the word *cowboy* was becoming as empty of meaning as *villain* or *superhero*.

Obviously, I needed to look at older images of the cowboy in order to reestablish a solid sense that there was something more to being a cowboy than wearing a Ralph Lauren shirt. I began by studying books on the work of the two most famous western artists, Frederic Remington and Charles Russell. My reaction to their art was that I often liked their sculpture for its energy and spirit, but I felt that their paintings were ultimately disappointing. What comes out of the work of these two men is not so much a true record of the cowboy as it is scenes of theatrical heroism and stoicism. I had to keep looking for an authentic picture of the West.

When I found the photographic book *Life on the Texas Range* by Erwin E. Smith, I realized that what I had wanted all along were images of the cowboy's real work existence without all the bombast and aggression of his role as an Indian killer and outlaw. In Smith's photographs, I found something I could believe— the cowboy sat on his horse and watched cows, he ate his meals, he lassoed calves and branded them, and he did all this with cer-

1

2

3

4

5

6

tain dignity and reserve under a huge sky and amid spectacular scenery. Smith was a keen observer of the cowboy, and his photographs reveal a fine sensitivity to the light and atmosphere of the Texas range.

I chose one of them as the basis for my first painting: a couple of cowboys rounding up a herd amid a huge cloud of dust. I added figures from other photos to bring the shape into the long horizontal I needed. The painting was full of time-consuming details, and at the end of the third day of working on it, I realized that the color was inconsistent and the foreground riders, which I had added, did not convincingly sit in the same space as the other figures. Somehow I had moved too far from the mood that had first attracted me to the Erwin Smith photograph, and I had kept changing my mind about how I would evoke the color of such a sun-drenched, dusty day. After my typical crisis ritual of reducing the painting to a ghost by letting water from the tap run over it and then repainting areas of the picture with stronger color, I still wasn't pleased with the effect. I decided to leave the job alone for two days and start again later.

On one of my two days off, I was in a favorite used-book store looking through a rack of old art-exhibition catalogs. I found two catalogs which gave me fresh ideas for the Poco paintings. One was a group-show catalog of painters of the Southwest, the so-called Santa Fe painters, and the other catalog contained reproductions of three extraordinary Maurice Prendergast watercolors that I had not seen before. The Santa Fe paintings, in their rich, deep palette, inspired me to think about light in the desert in a different way, and the Prendergast reproductions focused my longtime interest in this artist on certain aspects of texture in his paintings that I had never felt so keenly before.

The Santa Fe paintings helped me see that although bright sun has a tendency to bleach out the colors of objects it shines upon, the idea of the sun and the light it produces is of a certain kind of visual richness. The Santa Fe paintings suggest that under its dusty, blinding surfaces, the material of the desert is being regenerated by the sun; the bright color used by these painters is an expression of this abundance of energy.

The Prendergast reproductions also made me realize something about energy. Although it had always been obvious to me that the puddles and daubs of Prendergast's watercolors were fundamental to the character of his style, it suddenly became clearer to me that it was the agitation of almost the whole painting surface that gave his paintings their unique energy. I saw that in my own work I could be more daring in breaking up large areas, such as skies or simple ground surfaces, than I had been. I went on to do the painting for the Poco album of songs by Richie Furay, which has a vitality inspired by Prendergast.

The second of the Poco paintings is based on a photograph by W. G. Walker that I found in the Time-Life book on the cowboy. I think that the success of my final painting is due in large part to how powerful and satisfying I found this picture of solid figures concentrating on branding a cow. Everything about the photograph satisfied me: the scale of this tableau, the mystery of bent heads, the delicacy of the dust rising in the middle of the scene. I was completely focused during the painting process itself, which had a special simplicity and intensity for me. The painting holds together particularly well, I think, and the figures successfully evoke the tension of difficult physical work. Somehow, the pieces of the painting add up to more than they should, and this "greater sum" is still a riddle to me.

7

8

10

9

POCO
THE SONGS OF RICHIE FURAY

11 | The photo that inspired the second Poco painting.
12 | The front jacket as it was printed.
13 | The finished painting.

13

11

12

Number 1 Cover

Summer 1981
Sports Graphic
AD: Hidesuke Matsuo

1 | Original sketch sent to the client in Japan.
2 | Art director's notations which, I was assured, simply asked that the gymnast be removed and suggested compositional positions for the diver.
3 | Research photo from the 1930s.
4 | The finished painting.

I have always distrusted too much simplicity. I know that, visually speaking, it is the most logical and effective way to make dramatic graphic images, but there is something in me that wants to complicate things, to give them nuances and second levels, to describe the visual equivalent of "and then . . ." or "what if . . . ." I don't really like painting big heads or big anythings that dominate space, and it is very hard for me to reduce my imagery to one figure, big or little. On the occasions when I have done it, I usually have tried multiple-image solutions first or have felt the implications of the single subject were sufficiently complex.

I am not always right in this instinct. Sometimes less is more and bigger is better. In the case of this cover for the Japanese sports magazine *Number 1,* for which I sketched a diver and gymnast, the client asked me to leave out the gymnast and redesign the cover around the diver alone. The client was right. Not only was I making a play between two differently airborne figures that was too subtle to matter, but also the art director saw that the diver was more interestingly painted than the gymnast. He had made a good intuitive choice, for the truth was that I remember being slightly bored with painting the gymnast after the juicy color game of the diver's glistening skin. When I saw the art director's sketch and notations, however, I was understandably concerned that they had found a great deal wrong with my comp. Fortunately, Kaede Seville, who acted as the magazine's representative in New York, was able to assure me that the only changes I was being asked to make were deleting the gymnast and repositioning the diver slightly off-center.

Ironically, the research for the diver came from an unidentified magazine photo (probably from a 1930s European publication), but the gymnast was chosen from a number of photos I took myself after making some complicated arrangements to get a press pass to the American Cup gymnastic meet. After my having made the effort to attend this event and take photos especially for this magazine cover, it was surprising that my first sketch was not more exciting; however, the difference in the way I painted the two athletes may have to do with the fact that my conception of the diver had been vitalized by a TV special I had just seen on Leni Riefenstahl and her film *Olympiad.* The way she used camera angle and lighting to classicize the athletes in her film on the 1936 Olympics, particularly the divers, had stuck in my mind. The photograph I found of the man diving had something of the same classic but moody quality of the Riefenstahl film. The gymnasts I had seen and photographed, on the other hand, had been performing within a sterile jungle of equipment and the almost shadowless lights of Madison Square Garden. At another time I might have made better use of the machinelike atmosphere of the gymnastic competition, but in this period the romantic classicism inspired by Riefenstahl suited me better.

When it came time to do the finished painting, I really enjoyed the deeper color with which I was experimenting for skin tones and the dramatic effect of the bluish green shadows. Not only did these shadows increase the color vibrancy of the whole figure, but they also helped to connect the figure to the green water beyond. In my finish, I decided to evoke the water with more squiggly, calligraphic shapes than I had with the sketch—influenced, probably, by the idea of Japanese art. Once I had seen the possibilities of the cover as a very simple and dramatic image, I wanted everything, including the water, to work decoratively as well as realistically.

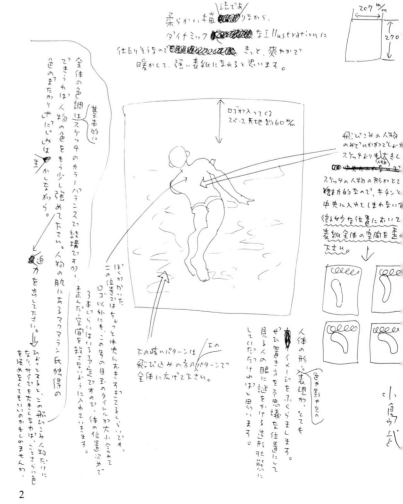

2

4

Whiskey Sour

1981 calendar
HBA; Dai Nippon Printing Co.
AD: Shinichiro Tora

There was a hard-to-believe quality about this assignment from the start. The client was the Hotel Bartenders Association of Japan, which is a novel enough idea for a group, but the organization is also surprisingly large, rich, and able to produce a big color calendar every year using expensive illustrations from all around the world. Not only that, they assign the paintings for each month by simply giving the artist the name of a drink and saying, "Paint anything it makes you think of."

The drink I was asked to illustrate was the whiskey sour, and my first thoughts about it were that, although whiskey is a tough man's drink, the "sour" part of it is complicating and feminizing. I also saw it, as I do many cocktails, as a drink belonging to the era of Fred Astaire and cruises on Cunard Liners.

When I mused on the possible visual direction I could follow to capture the spirit of the cocktail, I remembered an old 1930s postcard I had bought some time ago at a flea market in Sag Harbor. Actually, it was one of three postcards I had purchased that depicted life in the U.S. Navy. One of them shows a wrestling match aboard ship, a second card shows sailors boxing, and the third portrays a shipboard musical group. These cards are based on candid, inexpertly taken black-and-white photographs. The fact that they were then tinted in colors like aqua and peach did very little to relieve the basically smudgy quality of their printing or to romanticize the entirely honest view of the sailors they present. Their appeal is in their slice-of-life reality and the mystery of why they were reproduced in the first place. It is hard to imagine a sailor sending his sweetheart a postcard of two of his shipmates wrestling, particularly if the men look more like clumsy off-duty bakers than they do champions of the navy.

The card depicting a small musical group squatting and sitting near a gun turret evoked that quality of innocence one tends to ascribe to the past, which I remembered from the photographs taken by my parents in China in the thirties. The town we lived in, Chefoo, was for a number of summers a host port to the American navy, the so-called White Fleet which toured the coastal cities of China in a gesture of friendship and strength. The officers and men of the ships provided the July seasoning for the parties and dinners of European society in places like Chefoo. My parents' snapshots of officers lounging on the rattan chairs of our porch are much more decorous than the flea-market cards, but some simplicity in the men's gazes marks them as being from the same era as the sailor musicians.

My idea for the whiskey sour painting uses the sailors from the musical postcard, who perform as background minstrels or maybe as stunned onlookers to a woman in the foreground who leans voluptuously on a bar. The woman orders a whiskey sour or perhaps simply poses a riddle for the calendar viewer. My wife acted out the role of the mysterious bar lady, sometimes accompanied in her languorous gesture by Ogden, our parrot.

Because I chose a pose in which the face is dramatically backlit, I worked through five paintings in order to resolve the problem of painting the shadowed face in bright, expressionistic color. It meant painting wet color into wet color to achieve fluid transitions and finding combinations of blues, greens, oranges, and pinks that would work. I also wanted the drawing to be very simple, and so I reconstructed the sailors in my mind as primal figures. Every once in a while I do a painting which feels like an opening up of possibilities. What I achieved for myself in this painting was a step further in my experiments with brighter color and a simplified, more cubistic breakdown of form.

U. S. Sailors Life "Music on Deck"

1

2

3

134

4

5

6

7

8

Graphis Cover

June 1981
Graphis Press Corp.
AD: Walter Herdeg

Every carte blanche assignment comes with subtle baggage that I have to deal with and that in one way or another influences the creative choices I make. When Walter Herdeg, editor of *Graphis* magazine, invited me to design a cover for an issue that contained an article on my work, the unspoken "baggage" attached to this assignment was the need to respond to the character of the magazine itself—what kind of a cover is right for *Graphis*?

It is difficult to pin down the personality of a magazine in so many words. In the case of *Graphis*, I could say that it is European, that it is the oldest of the graphic magazines, and that in my mind it is somehow more connected to the traditions of poster making than it is to advertising or magazine illustration. However, all of this is a little vague, and when I started to sketch ideas for the cover, I found it was more useful to simply look at covers from past issues. What I saw were many strong, poster-esque ideas that were rendered with emphasis on the movement of the human hand—bold, calligraphic drawings, rough-hewn shapes, or slightly scratchy drawings that made me think of the artist at work. This quality gave *Graphis* covers a certain warmth whatever the nature of their ideas.

Recognizing simplicity as a typical virtue of *Graphis* covers didn't prevent my trying a complicated idea (after all, knowing the expectations is often just a preamble for resisting them). I had, in the process of solving a previous job, photographed my Burmese cat sleeping contentedly in a wicker chair. Although on this other occasion I had decided not to use the image, I was still fascinated by the scene of the light falling through the wicker of the chair, warming up the cat, and illuminating the design of the Oriental carpet on the floor. Although the sketch I made of it as a *Graphis* cover has a certain charm and derives graphic drama from the strong pattern formed by the light, I finally decided it was too much of a non sequitur—the idea didn't attach strongly enough to my own work, to graphics in general, or to some important issue.

After playing around with sketches of my six-month-old daughter, Leigh, as a cover girl, I decided to look outside the arena of my domestic life for my idea. Through some labyrinthine series of connections, which started with my pondering water colors and water subjects, I struck on the idea of a water pistol. It was interesting to me because the toy is a benign version of a dangerous weapon and because it uses the same kind of "ammunition" that I use in my work. My first version of the water pistol cover was a parody of the scene in the legend of King Arthur in which the sword Excalibur is lifted out of a lake by a mysterious hand. In my version, the sword is replaced by a water pistol shooting a jet of water that spells out the word *Graphis*. After buying four different water pistols at the local Woolworth's and studying them, I realized it would be much more interesting to use a painting idea that would let me explore the transparent structure of a plastic water pistol than to carry out my hand-in-the-lake concept. I set up a yellow-green plastic pistol on a target shape and proceeded to paint it as a still-life subject. Originally, I had thought it would be provocative to cover the target with blotches and streaks from the pistol, but the more I studied the effect of the light moving through the transparent plastic and the water it contained, the more I became intrigued with the light refractions in the gun and the glow of yellow light around it. I decided that the streaks on the background would be a distracting texture to both the yellow glow and the word *Graphis*, which I had positioned to suggest markings on a target.

1

2

3

4

5

6 First pistol idea, with gun squirting out title lettering.
7 Pencil sketch of final pistol idea.
8 Photo of water pistol.
9 Color sketch.
10 Finished art.

6

7

8

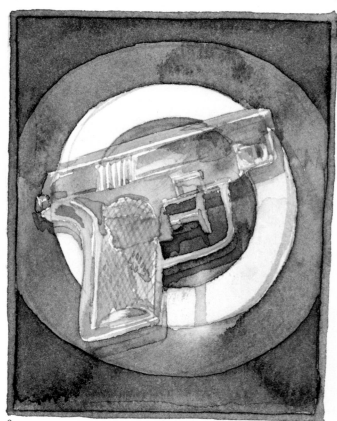

9

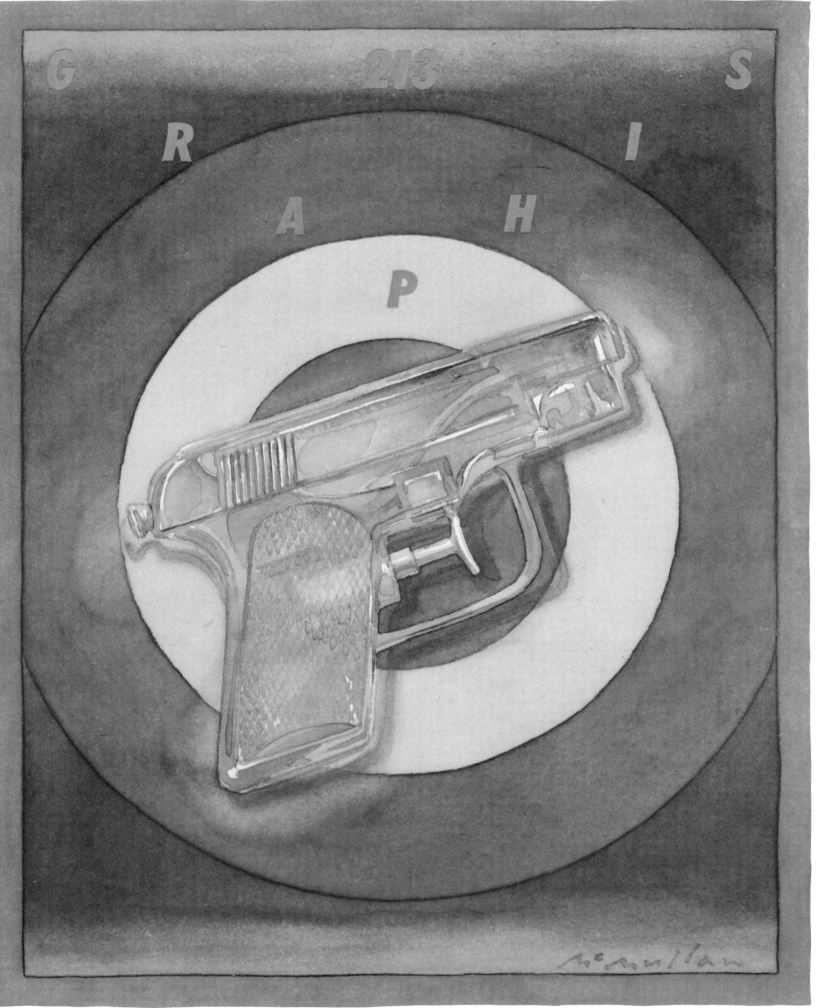

Index

Page numbers in italics indicate illustrations.

Edited by Michael McTwigan and Betty Vera
Designed by James McMullan
Mechanicals by Robert Fillie
Graphic Production by Hector Campbell
Text set in 9-point Times Roman